CREATING BRAVE SPACES FOR LGBTQIA+ STUDENTS

CREATING BRAVE SPACES FOR LGBTQIA+ STUDENTS

Five Keys to Schoolwide Belonging and Safety

CRAIG AARONS-MARTIN

iste+ascd
Arlington, Virginia USA

iste+ascd™
2111 Wilson Boulevard, Suite 300 • Arlington, VA 22201 USA
Phone: 800-933-2723 or 703-578-9600
Website: iste-ascd.org • Email: memsupport@iste-ascd.org
Author guidelines: ascd.org/write

Richard Culatta, *Chief Executive Officer;* Genny Ostertag, *Managing Director, Book Acquisitions & Editing;* Susan Hills, *Senior Acquisitions Editor;* Mary Beth Nielsen, *Director, Book Editing;* Megan Doyle, *Editor;* Lisa Hill, *Graphic Designer;* Valerie Younkin, *Senior Production Designer;* Cynthia Stock, *Typesetter;* Emily Reed, *Senior Director, Publishing Operations;* Christopher Logan, *Senior Production Specialist;* Shajuan Martin, *E-Publishing Specialist*

PAPERBACK ISBN: 978-1-4166-3453-9 ASCD product #125015 n6/26
PDF EBOOK ISBN: 978-1-4166-3454-6; see Books in Print for other formats.
Quantity discounts are available: email programteam@ascd.org or call 800-933-2723, ext. 5773, or 703-575-5773. For desk copies, go to www.ascd.org/deskcopy.

Library of Congress Cataloging-in-Publication Data

Names: Aarons-Martin, Craig author
Title: Creating brave spaces for LGBTQIA+ students : five keys to schoolwide belonging and safety / Craig Aarons-Martin.
Description: Arlington, VA : ISTE+ASCD, [2026] | Includes bibliographical references and index.
Identifiers: LCCN 2026010871 (print) | LCCN 2026010872 (ebook) | ISBN 9781416634539 paperback | ISBN 9781416634546 pdf
Subjects: LCSH: Sexual minority students—Social conditions | Belonging (Social psychology) | School environment—Social aspects | Inclusive education | Educational leadership
Classification: LCC LC2574 .A27 2026 (print) | LCC LC2574 (ebook)
LC record available at https://lccn.loc.gov/2026010871
LC ebook record available at https://lccn.loc.gov/2026010872

35 34 33 32 31 30 29 28 27 26 1 2 3 4 5 6 7 8 9 10 11 12

CREATING BRAVE SPACES FOR LGBTQIA+ STUDENTS

Foreword

As I write this foreword, we are living through what many describe as an unprecedented assault on the dignity and humanity of LGBTQIA+ people—particularly youth. More than 1,000 anti-LBGTQIA+ bills have been introduced across state legislatures in 2025 alone. These are not merely abstract policy debates happening in distant capitols. These are deliberate attempts to legislate our children out of existence, to criminalize care, to censor truth, and to force educators into silence. The stakes could not be higher.

But here's what I know to be true: legislation has never been enough to break us. Our people have survived—and thrived—through far worse. We have always found ways to create spaces where our children can see themselves, name themselves, and become themselves. This work, the work that Craig Aarons-Martin has poured into these pages, is an act of radical love and resistance in a moment that demands both.

I first encountered Craig's work years ago as the first executive director of the White House Initiative on Educational Excellence for African Americans under President Barack Obama and his brilliant wife Michelle Obama. Even then, I recognized in him a kindred spirit—a Black same-gender-loving/queer educator who understood that our liberation is bound up with the liberation of every child in every classroom. Someone who knows that when we fight for the most marginalized among us, we create conditions where everyone can flourish.

Throughout my career—from elementary school classrooms in New York to the halls of the U.S. House of Representatives and Senate, to the West Wing, to the National Black Justice Collective—I have worked at the intersection of policy and practice. I have seen how laws written in legislative chambers land in school hallways. I've written some of these laws. I have witnessed how a governor's signature on an anti-trans bill translates into a child's suicide attempt. I'm actively working to ensure Black LGBTQIA+ and same-gender-loving (SGL) students have access to free, high-quality mental health services. I have also seen how one brave teacher, one courageous administrator, or one committed youth worker can literally save a life.

Each of our students deserves to thrive, which is why Craig's framework matters so profoundly. The BRAVE principles—belonging, respect, advocacy, visibility, and empathy—are not feel-good platitudes. They are survival tools. They are democracy-preservation strategies and the practical manifestation of what James Baldwin meant when he said that freedom is not something that can be given but something we must take.

Let me be clear about something that Craig understands deeply: spaces cannot be safe if people do not feel they can be brave. For too long, we have settled for the language of "safe spaces"—as if our goal is simply to avoid harm and create bubbles where brutal truths can be ignored. But safety without courage is just another form of silence. And silence, as Audre Lorde taught us, will not protect us.

Brave spaces demand that we take risks. They require us to stretch, to grow, to do the uncomfortable work of unlearning what white hegemony, heteronormativity, homophobia, transmisogynoir, xenophobia, and anti-Blackness have taught us about whose lives matter, who deserves what we call justice or an opportunity to succeed in our global 21st century workplace, and whose stories deserve to be told. Brave spaces ask that we show up imperfectly but consistently, that we stumble forward even when we are afraid, and that we teach the babies—*all the babies*—even when powerful people threaten our jobs, our funding, and our very existence.

I want to speak directly to the educators, administrators, youth workers, and community partners who will read this book. You are not reading this by accident. You picked up this text because, somewhere in your spirit, you know that what we are doing to queer and trans youth—particularly Black,

Brown, and multiply marginalized young people—is unconscionable. You understand that the attacks on critical race theory, gender-affirming care for all, inclusive curricula, and recognition of a woman's right to bodily autonomy and the existence of LGBTQIA+ identities are all connected. They are part of the same project of control, the same tyranny of wealthy, power-hoarding elites who would rather see our children suffer than share resources, recognition, and humanity.

So what do we do? We do what our ancestors did. We organize. We resist. We build. We teach.

This book gives you the tools to do precisely that. In these chapters, you will find research that validates what your heart already knows. You will encounter stories that mirror your own struggles and inspire your courage. You will discover practical strategies that you can implement tomorrow—not someday, not when conditions are perfect, but now.

Here's the truth that Craig and I both live by: Our children cannot wait. They cannot wait for the Supreme Court to do the right thing, for Congress to pass the Equality Act, or for their states to repeal discriminatory laws. They should not have to wait. They need us to show up for them today, in this moment, with all of our imperfections and all of our power.

Some of you reading this are afraid. You are worried about losing your job. You are concerned about parental backlash. You are exhausted from fighting battles that seem endless, and perhaps, from your vantage point, unwinnable. I see you. I honor that fear. But I also want to remind you of something: Fear is data, not destiny. It tells us what we care about. It does not tell us what we must do.

We must defend democracy; protect schools from those who would privatize them, censor them, and weaponize them against our most vulnerable students; and create brave spaces where every child—regardless of who they are, who they love, how they identify, or what they believe—can learn, grow, and thrive.

This is not simply about LGBTQIA+ youth. It is about all of us. When we center the experiences of Black and Brown queer and trans young people—those who sit at the intersections of multiple forms of oppression—we create educational environments that work better for everyone. When we practice the principles of belonging, respect, advocacy, visibility, and empathy, we model the kind of world we want to live in.

I have spent my life trying to live up to the motto in my email signature: "Teach the babies (and the adults too!)." It is a call to action and a reminder that education is not neutral. Every day that we step into classrooms, board meetings, community centers, and policy spaces, we are either reinforcing systems of oppression or dismantling them. There is no middle ground.

Craig has given us a roadmap for choosing liberation, love, and courage. The question is whether we will use it.

As you read these pages, I invite you to sit with your discomfort, to interrogate your own biases and blind spots, and to consider the ways you have been complicit in harm, even unintentionally. And then I invite you to commit—not to perfection, but to action. Not to have all the answers, but to ask better questions. Don't wait until you feel ready, but start now. Consider the National Black Justice Collective a resource, www.nbjc.org, as you do this vital work.

The children are watching. They are watching to see if we will choose silence or solidarity. They are watching to see if we will prioritize comfort over justice. They are watching to see if our love for them is louder than our fear.

Let them see us choose bravery. Let them see us create spaces where they can breathe, dream, and become. Let them see us refuse to abandon them, even when—especially when—it costs us something.

This is the work, this is the calling, and this is how we bend the arc of history toward justice.

Craig Aarons-Martin has written a love letter to our community and a battle cry for our movement. Receive it as both. Honor the tenderness and embrace the urgency. Then we go forth and create the brave spaces our children deserve.

The future is counting on us. Let's not let them down.

In solidarity and with revolutionary love,

Dr. David J. Johns
CEO & Executive Director, National Black Justice Collective
Inaugural Executive Director, White House Initiative
on Educational Excellence for African Americans

Introduction

> "Love takes off the masks that we fear we cannot live without and know we cannot live within."
>
> —James Baldwin

A Moment That Shaped My Career as a Brave Educator

In the gentle hum of a Northeast independent school's community room, where the energetic rhythms of teenage life pulsed through the air—homework being scribbled, music flowing from headphones, and spirited conversations unfolding—a singular moment of vulnerability found its way to my doorstep. As a former history of immigration teacher turned dean of students, I navigated these halls with a keen awareness of the silent battles many of our students fought daily. That day, one such battle came to a head when a student I taught the previous year sought me out for a private conversation.

This young man, just on the cusp of adolescence at 14, was a vibrant soul who loved fashion and music, embodying the essence of Black pop culture with a beautiful voice that could quiet a room. Yet, as he approached, his usual charisma was replaced by a palpable nervousness that drew him inward. We retreated to the relative privacy of the bedroom I shared with a colleague, a safe enclave from the buzz of the community room.

As he stood by the window, his gaze lost beyond the glass, the signs of his internal struggle became apparent—his calm demeanor interrupted by bouts of silence and sudden teary eyes. With gentle probing, he shared his burden: he was planning to visit his father that weekend and feared that his father had learned something about him that filled him with dread. The weight of his anxiety was palpable as he hesitantly disclosed, "Craig, I think I'm gay."

The room seemed to close in as he spoke, his voice a mere whisper, his hands expressive yet trembling. His fear was not just of rejection but of a profound misunderstanding by a father shaped by Southern Baptist beliefs, a man from a world where certain truths were harder to reconcile. The possibility that his twin sister might have inadvertently exposed his secret only added layers to his fear.

My own journey echoed in his words. Having grown up closeted, with a father also from the South and of the same faith, I understood all too well the complex dance of love and acceptance within such familial bonds. My father, though filled with love, had also wished that I wasn't gay, a sentiment born not from malice but from a lack of tools to bridge our differences.

In this shared space, I saw not just a student but a reflection of my own past struggles. This young man had chosen me, perhaps sensing a kindred spirit through our interactions or the unspoken empathy in my lessons and guidance. This realization underscored the profound responsibility we hold as educators—not only to impart knowledge but also to foster an environment of empathy, curiosity, and understanding, allowing students to feel seen and supported.

As the conversation unfolded, we navigated his fears and planned how he might approach the conversation with his father, emphasizing honesty and preparedness for any outcome. This encounter, like many others, reinforced the importance of creating "brave spaces" in schools—environments where students can express their true selves without fear. These trends reflect a growing openness and an opportunity for educators to build on this progress.

The Renaissance of the BRAVE Framework for Educators

That moment with my student stayed with me, quietly shaping my understanding of what it meant to lead with truth and courage. Years later, during my tenure as head of a school in Roxbury, Massachusetts—a 99 percent Black and Brown public charter school community—those lessons would collide with history. It was the first Trump administration, and the world outside our school walls was on fire. COVID-19 was dismantling our sense of normalcy. The murder of George Floyd had ignited a global cry for racial justice. The Black Lives Matter movement was both celebrated and vilified.

Our community was considering adopting the Black Lives Matter principles as a way of being. Yet one principle—"Queer and Transgender Affirming"—sparked visible hesitation among some staff. They worried how conservative parents of our preK–8 students might react. I didn't understand the tension—until a professional development session made it plain. When I responded, "I am unsure what the tension is here. As a Black queer and gay man . . . ," audible gasps filled the room. I paused, realizing that despite the six-by-eight-foot intersectional pride flag in my office, despite the flags I hung in our school's open atrium, my own identity was not public knowledge to many on staff.

That pause held a thousand unspoken truths. It held the memory of an early childhood learner—a Brazilian immigrant boy emulating the fierceness of his mother and grandmother during playtime—who learned early that certain kinds of joy and expression would be policed. It held the face of a mother who once cried in my workshop because her child was one medical procedure away from finally feeling at home in their own body, only to have gender-affirming care outlawed overnight by a governor's pen.

It held the names of people like Samuel Edmund Damián Valentín, a transgender man in Puerto Rico whose New Year's Twitter post prayed for a world without killings—only for him to be murdered days later. Like Jahaira DeAlto, a beloved Boston advocate, ballroom mother, and protector of children "whose rainbow sparkled too brightly," whose life was taken violently in 2021. Like Jordan Burnham, a 17-year-old athlete who jumped from a ninth-story window after feeling crushed by invisible battles. Like Denise, a high school senior navigating depression and the fallout of sexual assault in a home that could not hold her pain (Human Rights Campaign, 2021).

It held the stories of educators too—of a Texas art teacher suspended simply for acknowledging her wife and of Victoria Thompson, a middle school teacher in South Carolina afraid that one honest word could cost her her job (Will, 2020). These were not abstract headlines; they were reminders that queer, trans, and nonbinary people—and those who love them—are living, teaching, and raising children in a country where visibility can be a liability.

And in the middle of it all were the children—watching, listening, absorbing. Some were quietly testing the air to see if it was safe to exhale their truth. Others were already shrinking themselves to fit into spaces that did not fit them back. The conversations I was having—in staff meetings, with parents, with young people—made one thing painfully clear: "safe spaces" were never enough. Stickers on a door, rainbow cupcakes during Pride Month, or a carefully worded DEI statement might soothe the conscience, but they would not save lives.

We needed something more—a way to equip educators, leaders, parents, and community partners to stand shoulder to shoulder with those already targeted by laws, policies, and rhetoric designed to erase us. We needed a framework that called us to *belonging, respect, advocacy, visibility,* and *empathy*—not as abstract ideals but as daily practices of courage. The BRAVE framework was born from that urgency, forged in a time when silence was complicity and action was an act of love.

BRAVE Framework: A Roadmap for Revolutionary Educators Who Choose Light and a Little Magic

We are living in a time of both crisis and possibility. As of the summer of 2025, almost 600 anti-LGBTQIA+ bills had been introduced in U.S. state and federal legislatures—many directly targeting queer and trans youth in schools (Movement Advancement Project, 2024). In this reality, creating inclusive classrooms is not simply an act of allyship—it is an urgent, life-saving, equity-rooted intervention. "Safe" is no longer enough. We must be *brave*.

This book introduces the BRAVE framework not as a performative checklist but as a practice, a mindset, and a movement—a tool for reflection, resistance, and reimagination. It's designed to be felt in your bones, practiced in your hallways, lived in your curriculum, and held in the culture of your school, organization, or home.

This framework wasn't written from a distance. It was born from decades of experience as a Black, queer educator and school leader navigating systems not built for me. It is fortified by the stories of youth and educators daring to exist authentically. And it is grounded in the wisdom of researchers, practitioners, and community-based changemakers who've been doing the work long before this book existed.

Why This Framework and Why Now?

This is not just a framework for LGBTQIA+ inclusion—it's a framework for transforming education for all, particularly those pushed to the margins.

In affirming schools, research shows the following:

- A 91 percent increase in school connectedness for LGBTQIA+ students (GLSEN, 2024).
- A 39 percent reduction in suicide ideation when youth feel affirmed in their identity (The Trevor Project, 2023c).
- Higher academic achievement, increased attendance, and fewer disciplinary actions (Kosciw et al., 2022).
- Greater trust in teachers, leaders, and systems (Greytak et al., 2021).
- Stronger peer relationships and whole-school wellness (Paceley et al., 2020).

The ripple effects are real: When we center queer and trans youth, we build schools where all students—especially those who are Black, Brown, neurodivergent, disabled, undocumented, first-generation, or low-income—can thrive.

The BRAVE Framework: Five Principles of Transformative Practice

The BRAVE framework invites you to lead from the inside out—starting with your beliefs and extending into your classroom practices, school culture, and policy decisions. Each principle is both an educational stance and a human commitment.

The BRAVE principles—belonging, respect, advocacy, visibility, and empathy—are not static checkboxes to complete. The motion of the arrows in this framework (see Figure I.1) is intentional—it signals that we are constantly in motion, a work in progress, ever growing, being nurtured, and made stronger. This movement helps us bloom, blossom, and build deeper bonds with ourselves, our youth, and those we love.

FIGURE I.1
The BRAVE Principles Framework

To truly live these principles, we must also be willing to unearth. This means uncovering the learnings, beliefs, and stereotypes we've inherited or absorbed in our personal and professional development—and being ready to transform them. Dr. Gholdy Muhammad (2023), in *Unearthing Joy*, reminds us that

> To unearth is to engage in humanizing practices. We must return to earth, return to the land. We must unearth, which means to dig into the ground and bring excellence to light, to the sun. Unearthing requires digging, mining, and uprooting, and ultimately bringing genius to the surface, again to the sun. Revealing what has been pushed down and concealed, we must draw forth pedagogies of

> equity and excellence, moving students towards the sun, where they belong, moving students and educators towards genius and joy. (p. x)

She continues:

> Our students are flowers who desire natural growth and promises of the rain. They seek a rebellious bloom against control, authority, and convention that have not served them well, nor prepared them for the world. The elemental crush of society has not always centered their genius; it has instead focused on what they are not or cannot do. Yet, they grow—desiring environments that nurture their growth. (p. x)

This framework is one of those nurturing environments. It is a humanizing practice and pedagogy. Inside the classroom, outside in the community, and beyond the lives of queer and trans youth, the BRAVE framework helps us reverse harmful patterns and instead cultivate places where people can root deeply, grow fully, and move toward the light of possibility.

Belonging

As a Black, gay, cisgender male educator in America, I've spent much of my life navigating systems that weren't designed for me. I've been the only one. The first one. The one who didn't quite fit. My six-foot-three, dark chocolate frame wearing Air Force Ones, a Ralph Lauren blazer, and a Black Lives Matter T-shirt walks into a room and disrupts the air before I even speak. I've worn many masks. I've shapeshifted for safety. But at what cost?

In a world that often demands conformity and punishes difference, the absence of belonging can feel like erasure. Yet when we talk about belonging, we're not talking about fitting in—we're talking about being held in wholeness.

For queer and trans youth, the stakes are high. Studies like GLSEN's *National School Climate Survey* (2024) show that LGBTQIA+ students who report a sense of belonging are significantly more likely to attend school, engage academically, and feel hopeful about their futures. Without it, too many drift into despair. But with it? They fly.

This work is inspired by that truth—and by those who've built spaces of radical belonging long before the rest of the world caught up: people like Bayard Rustin, the openly gay advisor to Dr. King whose brilliance shaped the March on Washington, even as he was pushed to the margins. And Miss Major Griffin-Gracy, whose decades of advocacy for trans women of color is the embodiment of chosen family and community care.

My own journey began when I was 13, teaching multiplication to 3rd graders in a summer program. Ms. Madeline—barely taller than a car hood but mighty in her presence—handed me the chalk before I ever claimed my voice. She saw something in me I couldn't yet name. And in that moment, she created a space where I belonged. That classroom became my sanctuary. That affirmation became my origin story. That moment became a mirror of what we must give every child. Because when we belong, we bloom.

Respect

Respect means seeing someone's humanity and honoring it out loud. For queer and trans youth, especially Black and Brown youth, respect cannot be an afterthought. It must be a practice—a posture. It shows up in how we greet them, how we protect them, how we talk about them when they're not in the room.

I grew up in a world where masculinity was rigid and queerness was policed. Saturdays were for yard work and sports. Emotions were weakness. "Boy" had to mean one thing. Pink was suspect. Tenderness was suspicious. Respect was earned through silence and strength—not through truth. But what if we redefined respect not as compliance but as deep attunement?

What if we honored students the way Billy Porter demands space in a gown on the red carpet? The way *Pose* gave trans women like Mj Rodriguez center stage? The way Lil Nas X twerks on your expectations with glitter and gospel? These cultural icons are reminders that self-respect and external respect are intertwined—and revolutionary.

Respect also lives in quieter corners: the classroom where pronouns are used correctly, the hallway where a student is called by their chosen name without pause or question, and the staff meeting where policies are written with every child in mind.

Respect is not about agreement. It's about recognition.

Advocacy

Let's be clear: *neutrality is a myth.* In a time when over 600 anti-LGBTQIA+ bills have been introduced across the United States in a single year, silence is not safety—it's surrender. Our kids are watching. And they are waiting for us to be brave enough to fight for them.

Advocacy is about naming injustice. It's also about choosing love with your whole chest, lesson plans, library choices, school board meetings, and curriculum design. To advocate is to risk comfort for the sake of someone else's dignity.

We advocate not only because it's right but also because history demands it. From Marsha P. Johnson throwing bricks and joy at Stonewall, to CeCe McDonald defending her life and sparking a movement, to the parents marching in Pride parades holding signs that say, "I love my trans kid"—advocacy has always been how we move from survival to liberation.

In this book, you'll meet educators who don't just post rainbows in June—they disrupt policies, push systems, and speak the names others try to erase. They choose advocacy daily, because neutrality does nothing but keep injustice comfortably in place. So, let's stop asking, "Should I speak up?" and start asking, "How can I afford not to?"

Visibility

Visibility is both a practice and a promise—a sacred act of affirmation that tells every queer and trans student, "I see you. I value you. You belong here." And when that visibility is absent, it becomes its own form of violence. Invisibility is not neutral. It is intentional. From curriculum gaps to hallway silences, what is left unsaid often does the deepest damage.

When schools exclude LGBTQIA+ stories, when educators avoid using words like *gay, trans, nonbinary,* or *intersex* out of fear or discomfort, students notice. And they internalize those omissions as shame. That absence is loud. That silence is shaping.

Visibility means saying the names and telling the stories of queer and trans elders, youth, leaders, artists, educators, and freedom fighters. It means creating a kaleidoscope of representation that mirrors the fullness of our students' identities.

Visibility looks like

- Teaching the works of James Baldwin, Audre Lorde, and Essex Hemphill not just during Black History Month but year-round.
- Naming trailblazers like Sylvia Rivera, Miss Major Griffin-Gracy, and Kay Ulanday Barrett, who carved space for trans and nonbinary lives in the face of systemic violence.

- Reading books like *Felix Ever After* by Kacen Callender, *Julian Is a Mermaid* by Jessica Love, *Too Bright to See* by Kyle Lukoff, and *Last Night at the Telegraph Club* by Malinda Lo in English language arts.
- Displaying pride flags *and* Black Lives Matter signs *and* disability justice posters—because intersectionality is visibility.
- Including queer family structures in health class, showing drag artistry in art history, and naming ballroom culture as both creative and revolutionary.
- Celebrating staff and students who live in truth—queer teachers who model love without shame, trans students who change their names and thrive, allies who create safety with their voice and action.

Visibility is about presence, but it's also about power. It's about deciding whose stories shape the culture—and whose are edited out. We must also move beyond rainbow washing and surface-level gestures. Visibility cannot be performative. It must be protective, policy-rooted, and deeply relational.

You can't become what you don't see. But even more urgently: you can't *feel safe* in a place where your identity is hidden or forbidden. Visibility is not a bulletin board. It is a belief system. It is not decoration. It is a declaration that says, "Your joy matters. Your story matters. Your body, your name, your truth—they matter." And in a world that tells our students otherwise, that affirmation is not just brave—it's lifesaving.

Empathy

Empathy is not a soft skill—it's a radical practice. It's not just feeling sorry for someone. It's getting close enough to feel with them, to understand, to respond, and to risk being changed. In the context of queer and trans youth, empathy must be more than a talking point—it must be how we lead, teach, repair, and build.

This work will stretch you—it's designed to. It will confront you with questions about who you are, what you've believed, and where your silence has lived. But that stretching? That discomfort? That's where growth begins. That's where healing takes root.

Empathy is what allows us to move from defensiveness to accountability, from fear to curiosity, and from saviorism to solidarity. Consider the public journey of Elliot Page, whose visibility has helped millions understand the sacredness of transition, even in the face of vitriol. Think of Angelica Ross, who not only demanded justice on her own terms but also tirelessly educated others—building bridges between Hollywood, tech, and the trans community. Look to Jazz Jennings, who opened the hearts of a generation through honest storytelling. Or look to Donnie Cianciotto, whose work in queer and disabled theater invites us into deeper empathy across identities.

But empathy is not just about those in the spotlight. It's about the student who hasn't spoken all week, the colleague who's changing their name, or the parent afraid to share their child's truth at pickup. It's about choosing to lean in even when you don't have the perfect words. It's when a teacher revises their syllabus to include diverse voices or when a coach ensures every student has a safe place to change for gym—or when a principal advocates for gender-inclusive bathrooms, not as an afterthought but as a birthright.

Empathy is active. It's disruptive. It's reparative. It asks

- How do I show up when it's not convenient?
- Who am I centering in this decision?
- What have I been taught to fear—and what might I learn if I listen instead?

Empathy allows us to be imperfect and still committed, to be learning and still accountable, and to be human and still transformative. Queer youth don't need pity. They don't need fixing. They need systems that stop hurting them. Empathy is the soil where liberation grows. And if we want to create BRAVE spaces, we must be willing to get our hands in that soil.

An Invitation to Step into the Work

This book is not meant to sit quietly on your shelf. It is a book to be lived with, wrestled with, and carried into the spaces you lead and love. Some of you will read it cover to cover, taking in each story, reflection, and resource in sequence. Others may jump to the chapters that call most loudly to the needs of your moment—seeking a deeper examination, a deeper *unearthing* of yourself and your work.

However you enter, you are welcome here. This book is designed for individuals and for circles: teacher teams in search of a shared language, a Brave Educators Circle hungry for renewal, your personal Avenger Squad—those trusted co-conspirators on the front lines with you every day. Think of them as your cabinet of key advisors in building cultures of belonging and humanizing the people you serve.

The chapters are organized in three parts, each holding a piece of the BRAVE framework journey:

Part I: Foundations of BRAVE Leadership

- Chapter 1: Why Your BRAVE Leadership Matters Now More Than Ever
- Chapter 2: What We Need to Know About Sex, Gender, and Sexuality

Part II: The BRAVE Framework in Action

- Chapter 3: Building True Belonging in Our Classrooms and Schools
- Chapter 4: Respect Is a Two-Way Street
- Chapter 5: Advocacy Is a Verb
- Chapter 6: Visibility as Resistance, Ritual, and Refuge
- Chapter 7: Leading with Empathy and Humanity

Part III: Sustaining the BRAVE Work

- Chapter 8: How to Create Brave Communities in Hostile Times
- Chapter 9: Partnering with Parents, Caregivers, and Community Partners
- Chapter 10: BRAVE Forward: The Work is Ours Together

These chapters are not static lessons—they are invitations. You may read them in solitude, journal your reflections, or bring them to your team, your classroom, or your community. Each one holds reflection questions connected to the BRAVE framework—belonging, respect, advocacy, visibility, and empathy—so you can turn insight into action.

This is your framework. Your living document. Your map for returning, again and again, to the work of unearthing what has been buried, nurturing what has been planted, and building spaces where every person—especially queer and trans youth—can bloom without apology.

How Each Chapter Is Designed to Guide You

Every chapter in this book follows a rhythm—one that invites you to pause, reflect, and take action. Whether you are reading alone, with a trusted colleague, or alongside your Avenger Squad, each chapter is built to meet you where you are and move you deeper into the BRAVE framework.

Reality in View

We begin each chapter by grounding ourselves in a story or historical moment—what I call *snow globing.* Like shaking a globe and watching the flakes swirl, we pause to hold a moment still, turn it in our hands, and examine it from every angle. Research tells us that stories are not just illustrative—they are transformative. Neuroscience confirms that narratives activate more regions of the brain than facts alone, allowing us to connect emotionally and empathetically in ways that data cannot achieve by itself (Zak, 2015). And yet, in this moment in history, even our stories are under siege. For queer and trans people, the simple act of telling and preserving truth has become a form of resistance. Whether it's a single human account or a constellation of interconnected experiences, these opening narratives reveal the heart of the BRAVE principle we are exploring, naming tensions, illuminating epiphanies, and sparking shifts that forever change how we see—and act in—the world.

Rich in Research and Insights

From the first page to the last, the voices of brilliant thought leaders, past and present, guide our exploration. This includes not only scholarly work but also the data, statistics, and lived insights of queer and trans leaders who are fighting to keep our stories visible. We are in a moment where those stories, along with the data that affirms our existence, are being erased, removed, and pillaged from national clearinghouses and data centers. Hundreds of millions of dollars once dedicated to storytelling, data collection, identity protection, liberation work, human rights advocacy, and mental and physical health care for LGBTQIA+ communities have been stolen or dismantled by the Trump administration as part of the architecture of Project 2025—an agenda explicitly aimed at eradicating queer and trans rights, visibility, and support systems (Human Rights Campaign, 2025).

In this climate, it is an act of resistance to honor and uplift our thought leadership, our creative expression, and our cultural contributions. We draw from the legacies left to us in books, films, journalism, media, performance, dance, and every form of artistry and activism that has carried the truth forward. These voices are not just references; they are our inheritance, our archive, and our roadmap for sustaining and expanding freedom in the face of erasure.

Case Studies That Ground the Work

Educators often need to step into someone else's shoes to fully see the path forward—and not just to understand a student's challenges but to witness the courage, creativity, and resistance required to navigate them. Throughout this book, you will meet students, teachers, and community leaders whose stories are both mirrors and windows: mirrors that reflect our own biases, blind spots, and possibilities, and windows into lives and realities that may be vastly different from our own. Their journeys are not sanitized or stripped of complexity; they carry the fullness of joy, pain, resistance, and transformation. In times when queer and trans narratives are being deliberately erased from public record, these case studies serve as living counter-archives—preserving truth, affirming humanity, and modeling what it looks like to build liberatory, life-affirming spaces.

Key Takeaways and Reflection Questions

Each chapter closes with key takeaways and reflection questions—each one intentionally connected to the BRAVE principles of belonging, respect, advocacy, visibility, and empathy. These are not just prompts for "quiet thinking." They are invitations to interrogate your own beliefs, disrupt patterns that no longer serve, and consider how your leadership shows up in both moments of ease and moments of tension. Reflection is not a passive act here; it is an active, embodied practice. The questions are crafted to stretch you beyond your comfort zone into spaces where real transformation can occur—for yourself, your team, and the communities you serve. They are as much about reimagining the systems you work within as they are about deepening your human connections.

Digital Resources

Every chapter includes links to CCM Education Group's curated ecosystem of resources—music, videos, readings, and first-person stories that amplify the lived experiences of queer and trans youth and adults. These aren't "extras" or optional enrichment; they are a continuation of the work you will begin in these pages. In a time when digital archives and LGBTQIA+ resources are being stripped from public platforms and funding pipelines, these curated collections act as cultural lifelines—preserving and celebrating the artistry, scholarship, and humanity at the heart of this work. They are designed to immerse you in the fullness of queer and trans brilliance, resilience, and joy, and to ensure that the voices fueling your leadership remain accessible, alive, and impossible to erase.

This structure isn't accidental—it's intentional. We move from story, to insight, to action because transformation requires all three. When we see clearly, think critically, and act bravely, we become the leaders our communities deserve

Closing: You Are BRAVE—And This Work Is Ours

Let's be real: this book doesn't offer shortcuts. Liberation isn't a checklist. Healing isn't linear. Systems don't shift overnight.

But there *is* a way forward. There is a BRAVE path—one that helps us move from

- Trauma-informed to liberation-centered.
- Performative allyship to sustained, relational advocacy.
- Silence to radical belonging.

Dr. Gloria Ladson-Billings reminds us that culturally responsive pedagogy is not a technical strategy—it's a mindset. Dr. Bettina Love calls us to build schools that are not simply better but worthy of our students' brilliance. Dr. Zaretta Hammond teaches that rigor and relationship are not enemies—they are interdependent. This book stands on the shoulders of those truths and adds a distinctly queer, joyful, and unapologetic lens for action.

And make no mistake: This work is personal, not because my experience represents every queer or trans journey, but because stories have power. As a gay Black man, my path informs my perspective—but my voice is one among many. Do not make the queer or trans person in your life your only "teacher." It is your responsibility to seek knowledge, ask questions, and do the work. Start here, and remember—*Google is still free.*

Allyship is not a destination; it's an ongoing process of learning, unlearning, and relationship building. There will be moments when you are uncomfortable, when you get it wrong, when you feel the urge to retreat. Keep going. As ALOK Vaid-Menon, a gender nonconforming artist, reminds us, "The magic of queerness is transformation" (Marchese, 2023). Transformation is messy—but it is also beautiful and necessary.

The relationships you build with LGBTQIA+ youth, colleagues, and communities can be life-giving—for them and for you. Whether you are a seasoned advocate or just beginning, know this: you are not alone. This is a movement. And your presence matters.

Let this book be

- A mirror to examine yourself with compassion.
- A compass to navigate systems with clarity.
- A torch to light the way for others.

You are not just a teacher. Not just a parent. Not just a leader. You are a culture shaper. A barrier breaker. A liberation architect. You are BRAVE. Let's begin.

PART I

FOUNDATIONS OF BRAVE LEADERSHIP

1

Why Your BRAVE Leadership Matters Now More Than Ever

"We need in every bay and community a group of angelic troublemakers."
—Bayard Rustin

The Urgency of Now

We are living through a coordinated assault on the lives, identities, and futures of LGBTQIA+ youth—especially Black, Brown, and multiply marginalized young people.

At the close of the summer of 2025, over 600 anti-LGBTQIA+ bills had been introduced in U.S. state legislatures (ACLU, 2025). The U.S. Supreme Court has upheld Tennessee's ban on gender-affirming care for minors—setting a precedent for similar bans in 27 states and cutting off medically necessary care for thousands (Human Rights Campaign, 2025). Around 25 states are enforcing blanket bans on gender-affirming care, leaving over 100,000 transgender youth with interrupted access to life-saving medical treatments (Smallens, 2025). Nearly one-third of LGBTQIA+ students attend schools with at least one anti-LGBTQIA+ policy—particularly prevalent in the South—correlating with increased rates of anxiety, depression, and suicide attempts (The Trevor Project, 2024c). A national survey found that 39 percent of LGBTQIA+ young people seriously considered suicide in the last year—rising to 46 percent among transgender and nonbinary youth—and that 50 percent of those seeking mental health care couldn't access it (The Trevor Project, 2024c).

Each policy is a message: *You do not belong here.* And young people hear it.

- Approximately 41 percent of LGBTQIA+ youth seriously considered suicide. For Black LGBTQIA+ youth, this number is even higher, particularly for those who also face food insecurity or housing instability (The Trevor Project, 2023a).
- LGBTQIA+ youth who experience houselessness or food insecurity report significantly higher rates of anxiety, depression, and suicidality. For instance, more than 60 percent of LGBTQIA+ youth experiencing food insecurity reported frequent symptoms of depression, compared to 42 percent of those with stable access to food (The Trevor Project, 2023b).
- Positive affirming events, such as seeing LGBTQIA+ representation in media, receiving affirming messages from educators, or participating in Pride events, were strongly correlated with lower odds of attempting suicide among LGBTQIA+ youth (The Trevor Project, 2023c).

And yet, in a regressive political move, the Trump administration officially shut down the LGBTQIA+ specialized services within the 988 Suicide and Crisis Lifeline in early 2025—cutting off one of the few national resources tailored to the specific needs of queer and trans youth in crisis (The Trevor Project, 2025).

Further, the Supreme Court's June 2024 decision to uphold Tennessee's ban on gender-affirming care for transgender youth signals not just a legal precedent but also a cultural attack on trans existence (The Trevor Project, 2024b; National Black Justice Coalition [NBJC], 2024). As the NBJC declared, "This decision codifies cruelty. It is an act of political violence dressed in legal robes."

This is not theoretical. These are the lived realities of the students in your care—students walking through metal detectors and masking their identities in hallways, scrolling through news stories about laws that erase them, and wondering if their school is one of the few places where they'll be seen, heard, and loved.

And this is why your leadership matters.

Leadership that affirms queer and trans youth is not optional—it is *urgent.* In an environment of systemic erasure and targeted harm, your presence, your policies, and your pedagogy can be a life-saving intervention. You have the power to shift a student's trajectory—not just by what you teach but by *who you choose to be.*

A Classroom Closet with Cracks of Light

When I was a young teacher in southeast New Orleans in 2001, I didn't walk into my classroom "out." I walked in masked. Every day I carried the weight of invisibility—the kind you learn in childhood when silence is mistaken for safety and hiding becomes second nature.

My father was born in Mississippi, one of 13 children. He was a military man, a long-haul truck driver, and a strict disciplinarian. In his world, masculinity was defined by hardness, obedience, and emotional restraint. "The rod spoke more than the child," and deviation from the norm was corrected, not discussed. My queerness didn't just threaten my safety—it threatened a lineage of masculinity forged in survival and silence.

So I learned to keep it in—to code-switch not only linguistically but also emotionally. At school, I was "Mr. Martin," the warm demander. Organized. Energetic. Always ready with a firm word or a playful push toward excellence. I knew how to show up for my students. But I didn't yet know how to show up for myself.

And yet—my students *knew.*

They saw something in me, even before I had the language to name it out loud. I became a quiet refuge for the queer and questioning youth in my school—especially Black boys who didn't know how to talk to their fathers or who feared the very same rejection I carried in my bones. Some would linger after class just to talk. Others wrote me letters they never meant for anyone else to see.

A few even said it outright: "Mr. Martin, I think I'm like you."

In those moments, I felt both seen and afraid. I wanted to say more. I wanted to tell them they were not alone. But I was still learning how to believe that for myself.

Those young people taught me something I couldn't have learned from any professional development: Visibility is not about disclosure—it's about presence. It's about cultivating an energy where students feel safe enough to wonder, question, and speak, even if the adults haven't said everything out loud.

A Principal with Partial Visibility

Fast forward to 2013. I was now a principal in south Boston, navigating a new level of leadership. I wasn't as closeted anymore—but I also wasn't out in the ways I wanted to be.

I existed in a system that had made space—*safe* space—for white queer and trans educators. Their gender identity and sexual orientation, while still marginal in many ways, were protected by a layer of whiteness that buffered them from certain institutional harms. For me, a Black queer man in leadership, the stakes were different.

I had a seat at the table, but I often had to translate my truth to be palatable in that space. I was strategic. Measured. I played respectability politics in ways I didn't always name at the time. And while I championed policies that affirmed LGBTQIA+ students and staff, I still struggled to fully insert myself into the story.

I knew the cost of being visible. I had watched leaders of color be scrutinized more harshly, their competence questioned more quickly, and their missteps punished more severely. And I feared that my queerness would not be seen as an asset to school culture but a liability to be managed.

Still, I also knew what was at stake for my students.

There were trans kids navigating school bathrooms and hallway stares. Nonbinary students whose pronouns were ignored or mocked. Gay students who smiled brightly in front of classmates but wept in conversations with school counselors. And through it all, I knew: *they needed more than policy.* They needed BRAVE spaces.

What It Means to Be BRAVE

They needed spaces where belonging wasn't conditional. Where respect was more than tolerance. Where advocacy wasn't something we scrambled for after harm but a steady heartbeat woven into daily practice. Where visibility wasn't an act of defiance—it was the air we breathed. Where empathy didn't have gatekeepers, and every story—especially those at the intersections of race, gender, and sexuality—was held as worthy.

I didn't have to be "out" in every way the world expected in order to be BRAVE. But I did have to be intentional. I had to face the truth that building safety for others often begins with healing the fractures in your own story. Trauma doesn't dissolve when you take the mic or the corner office—it simply learns new disguises. And real leadership is not about preserving the spaces you inherited but creating the spaces you once prayed for.

Being BRAVE meant refusing the scripts I'd been handed by systems that were never built with me in mind. It meant beginning every day with two questions: "Who still feels unseen here?" and "What will I do about it?" It meant realizing that every hallway banner, every library shelf, every staff meeting, every family newsletter was a choice—a chance to signal belonging or to silently uphold exclusion.

Safe comes from the Latin *salvus*: unharmed, uninjured. Safety is protection. It's shelter from the storm. *Brave* comes from the Latin *bravus*: splendid, valiant—courageous in the face of danger. Safe spaces are where we catch our breath. Brave spaces are where we use that breath to speak, to act, to transform.

And in a time when laws, biases, and systemic inequities are working to erase our queer, trans, and racially diverse communities, safety alone is not enough. Safe is the floor. Brave is the ceiling.

This is the work. We must keep building that ceiling together, higher and stronger, until it becomes a sky wide enough for all of us to live, love, learn, and lead without apology.

Introducing the BRAVE Framework: A Justice-Centered Compass for Today's Educator

We are living in a time of escalating backlash—where authenticity is not only punished but legislated against. Across the nation, teachers and school leaders have been fired, doxxed, publicly attacked, or even had their licenses threatened for doing what, at its core, *should* be the minimum in human-centered education: honoring a student's pronouns, displaying a pride flag, using inclusive literature, or daring to exist as their full, queer, trans, or nonbinary selves.

This is not abstract or distant. These are real kids walking through hallways that may punish them for existing. These are real educators bracing for backlash for applying empathy, for teaching civics, for holding up a torn rainbow flag. Safe spaces are critical—but when systems are this punitive, safety becomes merely the baseline. That's why this moment demands BRAVE.

The BRAVE framework—belonging, respect, advocacy, visibility, and empathy—cannot live as a poster on a wall or a slide in a training. It has to breathe. It has to move. It has to guide decisions in moments when the stakes are high and the path is unclear. If it only exists in theory, it risks becoming another equity initiative that looks good in a binder but never changes the air our students breathe.

This is why the framework is presented here, not as an abstract ideal but as a living, adaptable tool—one that recognizes the realities of both restrictive and affirming environments and offers tangible, scalable actions for each. In schools where policy forbids a teacher from saying *gay* or using a student's pronouns, BRAVE work might be quiet, coded, and deeply personal. In schools where pride flags fly in every hallway, BRAVE work might mean pushing beyond symbolic gestures toward systemic transformation. In either setting, the question is the same: "What can I do today to expand safety into liberation?"

Figure 1.1 offers a practical lens for educators, leaders, and community members to do more than simply reflect on their values—it's a roadmap for planning, acting, and holding ourselves accountable to the changes we commit to making. For each principle of the BRAVE framework, you'll find a clear commitment statement, the common barriers or misinterpretations that can distort its meaning, and examples of how the principle can be applied in both restrictive and affirming learning environments. This approach ensures that, no matter your context, you can adapt the work to meet the realities you face—while still moving toward liberation.

How to Use the BRAVE Framework

The BRAVE framework is more than a set of values—it is a justice-centered compass and a decision-making map for anyone in education committed to the safety, dignity, and success of LGBTQIA+ students, staff, and

FIGURE 1.1

Conceptual Fluency of Multiplication Via the Skip-Counting Method

Principle	Commitment	Common Misinterpretations	In a Restrictive Environment	In an Affirming Environment
Belonging	Create spaces where LGBTQIA+ youth and adults don't have to earn safety—where their identities are not up for debate. Even in restrictive districts, belonging can live in your tone, your posture, and your policy advocacy behind closed doors.	*Misinterpretation:* Belonging = "fitting in" or assimilation. True belonging allows people to be fully themselves without masking.	Quietly affirm a student's identity in conversation, even if you can't display it publicly.	Co-create a student-led inclusion council to shape school culture and policy.
Respect	Respect is honor, not tolerance. It's using a student's pronouns even if your state says not to. It's refusing to let someone's humanity be erased by silence or politics.	*Misinterpretation:* Respect = politeness or "treating everyone the same." Real respect acknowledges and affirms differences.	Privately address a misgendering incident with a colleague using a nonconfrontational tone.	Implement gender-inclusive language in all official school documents and communications.
Advocacy	Speak truth, even when whispered. This might mean writing the equity memo others are afraid to write. It might mean pushing for policy shifts in staff meetings or creating healing circles after school.	*Misinterpretation:* Advocacy is only about big, public actions. Quiet, strategic interventions matter too.	Share LGBTQIA+ mental health research with a small leadership group to inform policy.	Lead a districtwide training or testify publicly in support of inclusive legislation.
Visibility	Visibility is risky—but it is also revolutionary. Maybe you can't display a pride flag on your door, but you can weave LGBTQIA+ authors into your reading list, model inclusion in how you speak, and build networks of solidarity inside and outside your school.	*Misinterpretation:* Visibility = only visual symbols. True visibility includes curriculum, leadership decisions, and narrative power.	Select an inclusive text for class and normalize it as part of the standard curriculum.	Host a Pride assembly or publicly identify as an LGBTQIA+ staff member in a school meeting.
Empathy	Empathy is not just "feeling" but *acting* with compassion. It means understanding the trauma that queer and trans youth carry, especially when their identities are criminalized, erased, or tokenized. Empathy is praxis.	*Misinterpretation:* Empathy is passive or "just listening." Real empathy requires informed, responsive action.	Provide a private check-in for a student who's been targeted by bias.	Facilitate a restorative conference involving students, staff, and families after an incident.

communities. It was designed to be adaptable, actionable, and measurable across roles and contexts.

- Teachers can use it to plan lessons, respond to incidents, and reflect on the subtle and overt messages their classroom sends about who belongs.
- School leaders can apply it when reviewing policies, setting expectations for staff, and determining how to respond publicly in moments of crisis.
- Counselors, social workers, and student support staff can use it to build trust with LGBTQIA+ students and families while advocating for systemic changes that protect mental health.
- District administrators can use it to audit curriculum, professional development, and communications for alignment with justice-centered values.

Figure 1.2 provides two scenarios for each principle—one for restrictive environments and one for affirming environments—because the realities educators face are not uniform:

- In restrictive settings, a teacher might risk discipline for displaying a pride flag, discussing gender identity, or including LGBTQIA+ authors in the curriculum.
- In affirming settings, the challenge may be complacency—assuming "We're already inclusive" and neglecting to push for deeper structural change.

By showing low-risk and higher-risk examples side by side, the framework ensures that

1. Every educator—no matter their political or cultural context—has an entry point for action.
2. BRAVE work remains contextualized, not watered down.
3. Growth is scaffolded—so a small action today builds toward bolder change tomorrow.

For those who may be at a foundational level of advocacy, Figure 1.2 presents a quick checklist that makes the BRAVE framework immediately usable. It offers a two-tier plan for translating principles into practice:

FIGURE 1.2
BRAVE Framework Decision-Making Flowchart

Empathy ➡	Empathy ≠ Passive Listening	Low risk: Private check-in ➡	This week: Reach out after harm event
		High risk: Facilitate restorative conference ➡	This semester: Embed trauma-informed practice
Visibility ➡	Visibility ≠ Symbols Only	Low risk: Select inclusive text ➡	This week: Add LGBTQIA+ voice to lesson
		High risk: Host a Pride assembly ➡	This semester: Embed trauma-informed practice
Advocacy ➡	Advocacy ≠ Big Actions Only	Low risk: Share mental health research ➡	This week: Share research with leader
		High risk: Lead districtwide training ➡	This semester: Partner with local organization
Respect ➡	Respect ≠ Politeness Only	Low risk: Address misgendering quietly ➡	This week: Correct misinformation once
		High risk: Gender-inclusive policy changes ➡	This Semester: Revise policy/form
Belonging ➡	Belonging ≠ Fitting in	Low risk: Affirm identity privately ➡	This week: Affirm one invisible student
		High risk: Student inclusion council ➡	This semester: Launch advisory group

- This week: one immediate, low-barrier action in each BRAVE area to maintain momentum.
- This semester: one longer-term, systemic change to commit to over time.

In professional learning settings, the checklist can be

- A reflection tool at the end of training, where participants document their "This Week" and "This Semester" commitments.
- A peer accountability plan where staff share progress during team meetings or coaching sessions.
- A living document (e.g., a Google Doc or shared bulletin board) updated and revisited throughout the year.

BRAVE Isn't Always Loud—But It's Always Present

Here's the truth many queer educators of color know: the risks are not theoretical. Being BRAVE may cost you. That's why this framework is not about performance—it's about sustainability. It's about staying rooted in who you are while doing the work. Some educators are in affirming schools where they can lead boldly, host GSA meetings, and bring queer joy into every hallway. Others are in schools where saying the words *trans rights* might result in a parent complaint or a superintendent call. BRAVE adapts to context, not to fear.

Being BRAVE might look like

- Supporting a student privately, even if you can't do so publicly.
- Organizing a book drive with inclusive stories off campus.
- Partnering with local LGBTQIA+ organizations to provide wellness support.
- Educating your school board with research before a harmful policy vote.
- Creating micro-communities of trust where brave conversations can happen.

You don't have to do it all at once—but you do have to start somewhere. This isn't just a framework. BRAVE is a way of being. It's a way of leading. It's a way to stay rooted in your why even when the winds of policy, politics, or pressure try to pull you off course.

It asks us to move from compliance to courage, from invisibility to intention, from safety to liberation.

And most important, BRAVE asks us to do this work together, because no one gets free alone. Not the students. Not the teachers. Not the principals. Not the parents navigating this terrain with their kids. To be BRAVE is to be unshakable in your love for yourself and your people—to be "cozy" in your own skin, unbothered by those who try to dim your light. It's the steady reminder that no policy, no threat, no whisper campaign can break your soul when your foundation is built on truth, joy, and unapologetic authenticity.

Whether you are a school leader creating systems of belonging, a teacher choosing what book to teach next, or a parent advocating at your school board—this framework is for you. You don't have to be perfect to be BRAVE. You just have to be committed. And when the weight of the work feels heavy, remember—your existence, your joy, your survival, and your leadership are already the revolution.

Key Takeaways

- **Liberatory leadership is urgent**—especially in a time when anti-LGBTQIA+ policies, book bans, and surveillance culture threaten the safety and belonging of queer and trans youth.
- **Being BRAVE means being visible.** Silence is not neutrality—it's complicity. Leaders must choose courageous visibility over comfort, even when it costs.
- **Queer and trans youth are watching how we lead.** Our decisions about curriculum, staffing, policy, and discipline shape whether they feel seen, valued, or erased.
- **Leadership grounded in the BRAVE framework offers a roadmap** for disrupting harm and building affirming school communities.
- **We are the mirror.** What we model as leaders—especially how we respond to discomfort, difference, and disruption—teaches others what is possible.

BRAVE Reflection Questions

Before you move on, take a few minutes to reflect—not just with your head but with your heart. Use the BRAVE framework as your compass. These five questions are meant to help you examine your leadership through a lens of identity, risk, allyship, and courage.

- **Belonging:** Who in your community is still navigating silence or shame instead of safety and belonging—and how can you shift that?
- **Respect:** What does it look like to respect someone's pronouns, identity, or story when doing so might put your role or reputation at risk?
- **Advocacy:** Where are you being called to speak up, show up, or disrupt harm for LGBTQIA+ youth—and what might you need to move past fear?
- **Visibility:** How does your presence—or absence—signal safety to queer and trans students and staff in your space?
- **Empathy:** What in your own story helps you understand the inner battles your students may be facing?

Chapter 1 Playlist

This chapter invited you to step into vulnerability, wrestle with history, and face the urgency of the present moment. Now it's time to extend that learning beyond the page.

Visit www.ccmeducationgroup.co to access a curated collection of articles, podcasts, videos, and classroom tools designed to deepen your understanding and fuel your action.

These resources are more than extra reading. They're conversation starters, mindset shifters, and practical guides to help you bring the BRAVE framework to life. Whether you're using them for personal study, as a team discussion tool, or to lead a professional learning session, each one is chosen to move you from insight to impact.

Inside this playlist, you'll find

- Historical and contemporary case studies of queer and trans leadership in education.
- Podcast episodes featuring frontline educators and students.
- Research summaries you can bring to staff meetings or school board presentations.
- Practical tools for implementing belonging, respect, advocacy, visibility, and empathy in your daily work.

2

What We Need to Know About Sex, Gender, and Sexuality

"How we present ourselves is language, reclamation, magic, joy, and power. Wear whatever you want. Break all the rules. Be all the genders."

—Addie Tsai

Language as a Tool for Liberation or Harm

Being BRAVE, as we explored in Chapter 1, is not just about what we do—it's about what we say. The stories we tell, the words we choose, and the silences we hold can be tools of liberation or weapons of harm. If our goal is to create spaces where every student feels seen, safe, and celebrated, then language is not a side note—it is the frontline.

This book is designed to be a resource and reflection space for you. I write as someone who has been both affirmed and silenced in school systems—someone who leads with both heart and history. Our students' understanding of who they are is constantly evolving. Every day they are renegotiating how they want to be seen and how they want to show up. To truly support them—and ourselves—we must meet that evolution with language that liberates, not limits.

Throughout this text, I use the acronym LGBTQIA, which includes lesbian, gay, bisexual, transgender, queer/questioning, intersex, and asexual, with the plus sign to leave it open for those who have more nuanced sexuality or gender presentations. This terminology continues to expand and shift, reflecting the rich diversity of identities within our communities. These identities also intersect with race, ethnicity, culture, religion, language, and ability—shaping the words we use and the meanings they carry. As you continue through this chapter, we will explore how these terms may show up inside and outside the classroom and how to navigate those intersections with care.

Let's pause for a moment on the word *queer*. Once used as a slur, *queer* was reclaimed in the 1980s by activists, particularly during the HIV/AIDS crisis, and has become a powerful umbrella term for people who do not conform to heteronormative or cisgender norms (Cheves & López, 2025). However, not everyone within the community embraces this term. Some feel it doesn't represent their experience or carries painful connotations. That tension matters—especially for educators trying to navigate respectful language. The key takeaway is to ask, listen, honor, and let the people in your care define who they are.

In education, words can create sanctuary—or spark trauma. The choice is ours. Language is not just semantics—it is systemic. It either maintains or disrupts the dominant narratives of who belongs and who does not. When we use a student's correct name or pronouns, we aren't being "politically correct." We are building trust. We are affirming their humanity.

So, before we move forward, take a moment: What words in your own life have made you feel like you belonged? And what words have made you feel like you were on the outside looking in? This is where our work begins.

My Journey: Silence, Shame, and Early Lessons on Language

Growing up in Catholic schools in New Orleans—a city overflowing with bold self-expression, glittering queer nightlife, and people who defied every expectation of gender and sexuality—I learned to stay silent. It was not because I didn't see queerness. I saw it everywhere: in the drag queens of the French Quarter, the butch lesbians on streetcars, and the flamboyant gospel singers on Sunday morning. But I also saw how people talked about them behind closed doors. I heard the slurs whispered at barbershops and cookouts. I felt the sting of judgment in my own home when anyone "acted funny" or didn't fit the mold.

At home, my father raised me and my brother with love, discipline, and a clear sense of what a "real man" should be. He taught us to work hard, repair what was broken, marry women, raise children, and live in service to God. There was no blueprint for being Black, queer, tender, and free. No permission to explore softness. No space for difference. To survive, I learned to smile when I was uncomfortable, nod when I disagreed, and keep quiet about who I was.

Even as I grew into my leadership as a young teacher and then a principal, I carried that silence like armor. I avoided conversations about gender identity or sexuality—not out of malice but out of fear and social conditioning. I struggled to use the correct pronouns. I deadnamed (using their birth name instead of the name they trusted me to honor) people without realizing the harm. I hesitated before affirming someone whose gender expression challenged my internalized norms. And if I'm honest, I often feared being seen in close community with queer or trans folks who were "too visible," afraid others might label me by association—afraid they'd call me a "sissy" or something worse and I'd lose the sliver of belonging I thought I had earned.

But silence isn't neutral. It's an accomplice to harm.

Years later, a student in my class pulled me aside. "Mr. Martin," they said, "you're the first adult who didn't look disgusted when I said I liked both boys and girls. That's why I trust you."

That moment cracked something open in me. I realized that affirming language isn't just about vocabulary—it's about liberation. It's about life and death. Our tone, our posture, our presence—they can either affirm a young person's humanity or reinforce the shame many of us were taught to carry.

From that day on, I began to unlearn. I started asking questions, listening more deeply, and making small shifts in my daily practice—choosing words that created safety instead of suspicion. The more I paid attention to language, the more I understood that it is one of the most powerful tools we have as educators to disrupt harm and build belonging.

Which brings me to Jay—a student whose story would force me, my staff, and our entire school community to confront whether we were ready to live out the values we claimed to hold.

Centering Jay: A Principal's Reckoning with Brave Inclusion

When Jay arrived at our preK–6 school in south Boston, he was quiet but sure of one thing—his name was Jay, and his pronouns were he/him. Fifth grade. He had a closely cropped fade, a beautiful and disarming smile, and a jawline just full enough that it made people pause. Some teachers whispered that he "looked like a boy," while others still stumbled over what they thought they knew: Jay had been assigned female at birth. But Jay wasn't confused. It was the rest of us who had to catch up.

The first alert came from my school secretary, Ms. Tasso—a woman of deep faith and even deeper love for children, who had been a cornerstone of our front office for decades. When she called me, her voice was laced with concern. "Mr. Martin, the district placed a new student with us—Jay. In 5th grade. They said . . . we should know he's transgender."

I took a breath. "OK," I said. "So what's the issue?"

There was a pause, and then the questions came tumbling out. "But what bathroom will he use? What name do we write in the files? What do I say if the aunt refuses to call him Jay?" They weren't just logistical questions—they were existential ones for a staff that had not yet faced the challenge of affirming a transgender child in real time, especially one who wasn't out to all adults in his life.

The tension didn't just sit in the office—it spread. Jay's arrival forced our community to reckon with how ready—or not—we truly were to practice the kind of inclusion we claimed to stand for. Jay's aunt, his legal caregiver, refused to call him anything but the name he was given at birth. She referred to him in the past tense, correcting staff and making calls to the school demanding to know why "Jenny" was being referred to as "he" in class. Her resistance wasn't just passive—it was a barrier we had to navigate daily. Every phone call, every family engagement event, every form sent home became a site of tension. It was exhausting. And necessary. I had to be clear with my team: Jay is not the problem. Our discomfort is.

As a Black queer man who had once feared being "found out" for simply sitting next to effeminate friends, I understood the fear of guilt by association. I understood how my secretary's religious upbringing clashed with the lived experience of a child like Jay. And I understood how exhausting it could be to constantly unlearn what you've been taught about gender, identity, and God. But I also knew what it felt like to be called something I wasn't. I knew what it meant to be silently erased—even when you were sitting in plain sight.

So, I met with my leadership team. I asked hard questions. What does it really mean to affirm someone, even when it stretches us? Are we brave enough to respect a child's identity in the face of adult pushback? Are we ready to make mistakes, be corrected, and still keep showing up? And we didn't just talk—we trained. We revised intake forms. We developed internal systems to ensure Jay's pronouns were used consistently without outing him to caregivers who didn't support his identity. We partnered with local LGBTQIA+ organizations for staff development. We rehearsed how to correct each other gently but firmly. "It's Jay. He uses he/him," became our default reminder—not just a correction but an affirmation.

Jay became a mirror—showing us the gap between what we believed and how we behaved.

For Ms. Tasso, it was a slow transformation. At first, she'd catch herself mid-sentence and shake her head, apologizing under her breath. But she kept trying. One morning, I heard her greet Jay with "Good morning, young man." Her voice wavered slightly, but Jay beamed. That moment mattered.

Every time we got it right, we helped Jay feel more fully seen. And every time we slipped and then corrected ourselves, we showed him that his dignity was worth the effort.

From Policy to Practice – Lessons from Jay's Journey

Jay's story illustrates a powerful truth: affirming a student's identity is not just about checking a legal box—it's about honoring their humanity.

When LGBTQIA+ youth walk into our classrooms, they are scanning for signals. *Will you say my name? Use my pronouns? Keep my truth safe? Or will you betray it in a moment of discomfort, gossip, or confusion?*

Here's what our team learned in real time:

- Affirmation needs a blueprint. Don't wait until a student transitions to review your intake forms, rosters, communication templates, and student record systems. Build affirming practices into your everyday operations so you're ready before the moment comes.
- Language is culture-shaping. Every word—whether in the front office, the hallway, or the classroom—sends a message. Students notice. Families notice. Staff notice. Decide which messages you want your community to absorb, and speak them consistently.
- Courage is contagious. When leaders model clarity, compassion, and follow-through, others begin to mirror it—even those who were hesitant at first. The tone you set will ripple outward.

These lessons didn't just help us support Jay—they reshaped the way we approached every student, family, and staff member in our building. They became the bridge between my own journey of silence and the kind of brave, affirming leadership I want every school to embody. And it starts with something deceptively simple: shared language.

Language as Liberation: Why Definitions Matter

Language is our most human technology. It builds trust. It sets norms. It liberates—or it harms.

In schools, language is never neutral. It's not just descriptive—it's prescriptive. It sets the tone for what is possible in a classroom, a hallway, or a leadership team meeting. The words we choose tell students, staff, and families whether they are fully welcome—or whether they must shrink themselves to fit someone else's comfort.

Jay's journey reminded me of something I had to unlearn: Language is not "just semantics." It's culture-shaping. It signals belonging. It creates (or erodes) safety. And it can make the difference between a student feeling empowered to speak their truth—or disappear into silence.

The challenge is that most of us were never formally taught the vocabulary of gender, sexuality, or identity. We're navigating evolving language with outdated tools—trying to teach for equity while still learning the words that help us lead with clarity and care. Too often, we rely on "safe" language that avoids offense when what our students deserve is *brave* language—language that names, affirms, and honors their lived realities.

That's why this chapter offers four core frames to examine

- Shared definitions to support clarity.
- The role gender norms play in how we build up or break down relationships.
- Myths and truths that challenge what we've been taught.
- Practical classroom strategies to apply what we're learning.

Let's begin by grounding ourselves in research-informed definitions that center dignity, agency, and affirmation. The definitions in Figure 2.1—aligned with the World Health Organization (n.d.) and Yale's Gender Program (Yale University, n.d.)—are not about "political correctness." They are about educational justice. They matter because the students and staff who embody them matter.

Why This Matters in Practice

Understanding these terms—and the human experiences they represent—is essential for fostering inclusion and belonging. Language is not neutral. It can plant seeds that bloom into affirmation or burn like wildfire when weaponized.

Used with curiosity and care—even if imperfect—language opens doors to connection. It tells a young person, colleague, or parent: *You are seen. You are valid.* But it can also send the opposite message, reinforcing shame, invisibility, or exclusion.

If we are serious about creating academic ecosystems rooted in equity, belonging, and justice, we must treat language as a core leadership skill, not an optional extra. This means

- Recognizing that language evolves. What's widely accepted today may shift tomorrow.
- Committing to ongoing learning. Educators, coaches, and leaders need safe, structured spaces to deepen their understanding.
- Applying language across contexts. From the bus ride to the classroom, from the parent meeting to the after-school program—students are listening for cues about their safety.

FIGURE 2.1

LGBTQIA+ Terms at a Glance

Term	Definition	Example/Context
Asexual	Experiencing little to no sexual attraction to others. May still form romantic, emotional, or intimate relationships	A person who has no sexual attraction but enjoys close romantic partnerships
Biological Sex	Physical traits (e.g., chromosomes, hormones, reproductive anatomy) typically assigned at birth	Someone born with XY chromosomes is typically assigned male at birth
Bisexual	Attraction to people of more than one gender	An individual attracted to both men and women
Cisgender	A person whose gender identity aligns with the sex assigned at birth	A person assigned female at birth who identifies as a woman
Female	Identifying with femininity or womanhood	A student who identifies as a woman and uses she/her pronouns
Gender Dysphoria	Clinically recognized distress when one's gender identity does not align with their sex assigned at birth	A person experiencing discomfort with their assigned sex seeks supportive counseling
Gender Expression	The external presentation of one's gender through clothing, hairstyle, voice, behavior, etc.	Wearing clothing typically associated with another gender
Genderfluid	A gender identity that may shift over time or in different contexts	A student who feels more feminine on some days and more masculine on others
Gender Identity	One's deeply held internal sense of being male, female, both, neither, or another gender	Someone identifying as nonbinary or genderfluid
Gender Nonconforming	A person whose appearance or behavior does not align with traditional gender expectations	An individual whose style challenges binary norms
Heterosexual	Attraction to people of a different gender	A man attracted to women
Homosexual (*less commonly used*)	Attraction to people of the same gender; some find this term clinical or outdated	A woman attracted to women
Intersex	Born with physical or genetic sex characteristics that don't fit typical binary definitions	A person whose chromosomes, hormones, or anatomy are not exclusively male or female
LGBTQIA+	Umbrella acronym: lesbian, gay, bisexual, transgender, queer/questioning, intersex, asexual, plus other identities	How someone might collectively describe diverse sexual orientations and gender identities
Male	Identifying with masculinity or manhood	A student who identifies as a man and uses he/him pronouns
Nonbinary	A gender identity outside the male/female binary	A student who uses they/them pronouns
Pansexual	Attraction to people regardless of gender	A person attracted across the gender spectrum
Queer	An umbrella term for identities outside heterosexual and cisgender norms; reclaimed by many as affirming	An educator who identifies as queer rather than a specific label
Two-Spirit	A term used by some Indigenous peoples for a sacred identity that blends masculine and feminine roles	A Native student embodying both traditionally masculine and feminine traits

As we explore gender, sexuality, and identity in this chapter, it helps to begin with shared language. Too often, schools and families stumble into conflict because we lack common definitions—or because we use the same words to mean different things. Here, we separate concepts that are often blurred together so we can talk with greater respect and clarity.

- **Biological sex** refers to physical characteristics—chromosomes, hormones, reproductive anatomy—typically assigned at birth as male, female, or intersex.
- **Gender identity** is a person's deeply felt sense of their own gender, which may or may not align with the sex they were assigned at birth.
- **Gender expression** describes how people outwardly express their gender through clothing, hairstyles, mannerisms, or names—and these expressions may or may not conform to cultural norms of "masculinity" or "femininity."
- **Gender** is a broader social and cultural construct that includes identity, roles, and expectations associated with being a man, woman, boy, girl, nonbinary person, or other gender identities across different societies.

For example, someone assigned female at birth (biological sex) may identify as nonbinary (gender identity) and use they/them pronouns while expressing themselves through clothing or hairstyles our culture labels as "masculine" (gender expression).

By anchoring ourselves in these distinctions, we create a common language for courageous conversations—with colleagues, families, and communities—about identities that have always existed but have too often been erased, misunderstood, or forced into boxes that don't fit.

The Early Lessons of Gender Norms

Even after spending more than 20 years as a public school educator, I can't walk into a kindergarten classroom without thinking back to my own childhood—those early, unspoken lessons about who I was *supposed* to be. The room might be filled with seemingly harmless objects—blocks, books, dolls, action figures—but these aren't just playthings. As scholars like Davis and Hines (2020) remind us, toys are social texts: they transmit powerful ideas about gender long before a child can define the word.

Looking back, I wonder: When did I first believe that certain toys "weren't for me"? When did I start editing my voice, my posture, and my clothing choices to fit an invisible script? These weren't explicit rules—they were subtle cues picked up from peers, parents, teachers, and the media.

Scripts from the Street

Take *Sesame Street*. It's rightfully praised for groundbreaking racial and cultural representation, yet early episodes also reflected gender norms embedded in their era. Big Bird could be silly, adventurous, and lovable—free to explore the world. Prairie Dawn, intelligent and capable, often played the role of organizer or nurturer, quietly managing the chaos. Researchers like Ditsworth (2001) have shown that even progressive children's media can reproduce gendered patterns, assigning "care" to girls and "quest" to boys.

These character patterns matter. When a boy only sees himself in Big Bird's playful antics and not in Prairie Dawn's leadership, or when a girl identifies with Prairie Dawn's kindness but never with Cookie Monster's unrestrained creativity, possibility narrows.

The Ambiguity of Teletubbies and the Anxiety of Adults

And then there's *Teletubbies*. In the late '90s, a wave of adult outrage swirled around Tinky Winky, the purple Teletubby who carried a bag. For children, it was simply a whimsical character in a whimsical world. For some adults, it became a flashpoint for anxiety about queerness and gender nonconformity.

This is a textbook case of what Renold (2004) calls gender policing—when adults, not children, draw rigid boundaries around what is "acceptable" for boys or girls. The panic wasn't about a bag—it was about the fear of what it might represent. And those fears filter into classrooms when educators, consciously or not, restrict play to protect a version of childhood that upholds binary norms.

The Influence of Hypermasculinity and Idealized Femininity

Cultural icons like *G.I. Joe* and Barbie have also left deep imprints. *G.I. Joe* embodied hypermasculinity: physical strength, stoicism, dominance.

Studies by Artz (2001) highlight how these ideals can limit boys' emotional expression and equate masculinity with control and power.

Meanwhile, Barbie has long reflected and reinforced idealized femininity—thinness, beauty, and perfection—as markers of worth. Even as Mattel has expanded Barbie's careers and body types, research (Artz, 2001) shows that early exposure to narrow beauty standards still correlates with lower body satisfaction and self-esteem among girls.

From Gender Norms to Gender Dystopia

Rigid norms aren't just limiting—they can become what I call *gender dystopia*: a deep dissonance between who a child knows themselves to be and who they're told they must be. For LGBTQIA+ youth, these constraints can fuel alienation and shame. They send the message that authenticity risks rejection.

This is compounded when the media punishes or erases characters who defy gender expectations or when adults project fear onto children's harmless self-expression. The Tinky Winky controversy shows that children's imaginations are rarely the problem—it's the adults' discomfort with breaking the script.

Reimagining Gender Norms in Today's Classrooms

Dismantling gender norms in schools isn't about letting girls play with trucks or boys play with dolls—it's about abolishing the binary thinking that labels any object, activity, or role as inherently male or female. That means

- Stocking classroom libraries with stories that show boys nurturing, girls leading, and nonbinary children being fully themselves.
- Choosing toys that encourage imaginative play without reinforcing stereotypes.
- Modeling inclusive language that doesn't sort children into "ladies" and "gentlemen" by default.

As Feeney, Freeman, and Schaffer (2019) argue, this work starts with educator self-reflection. We must examine the unconscious ways we uphold gender norms—in our praise, our discipline, our role assignments. It means challenging colleagues and families to see beyond "what boys do" and "what girls do."

When we shift from managing gender to expanding it, we move from containing identity to liberating it. And liberation requires more than good intentions—it demands dismantling the myths that keep these norms in place.

Naming What's False: Myths That Keep Us Stuck

Even with shared vocabulary, educators are still up against myths—social narratives passed down in teacher prep programs, family dinner tables, staff rooms, and state legislatures. These myths are often internalized so deeply that we don't recognize them as myths at all.

The most dangerous myths are the ones that go unnamed. They're not just misinformation—they're mechanisms of harm. When we say a child is "too young" to know their identity or that inclusive education is "political," we reinforce a system where only certain identities are seen as normal, neutral, or appropriate.

Let's start with Figure 2.2 to unlearn some of the most common myths so we can replace them with truth—and, more important, with liberating action.

FIGURE 2.2
Myths vs. Truths

Myth	Truth
Gender is binary.	Gender exists on a spectrum.
Sexuality is a choice.	Identities may evolve, but orientation is not a "decision."
Kids are too young to know their gender.	Many children understand and express their identities early in their toddler years.
Talking about LGBTQIA+ issues is talking about sex.	It's about so much more—identity, safety, and inclusion—not just sexual behavior.
Affirming students "encourages" them to be LGBTQIA+.	Affirmation reduces harm. Identity is not contagious—shame is.

From Myth to Environment

Myths don't just live in conversation—they show up in the way we arrange classrooms, the language we use, and the opportunities we offer. Every policy, poster, pronoun, and practice either reinforces restrictive norms or opens the door to affirmation.

When Gender Norms Meet the Classroom

In Ms. Reyes's 1st grade classroom, the art table was always a hive of creativity. One afternoon, Jay—an energetic boy who loved glitter—started working on a birthday card for his grandmother. He sprinkled gold sparkles over pink construction paper, carefully drawing flowers along the edge.

Another student, Daniel, glanced over and laughed. "That's for girls." The room went quiet. Ms. Reyes had a choice. She could redirect Jay to "more boyish" materials and avoid conflict, or she could name what was happening.

She chose the latter. "Colors don't have a gender, Daniel. Glitter is for anyone who likes glitter. What matters is that Jay is making something special for someone he loves."

In that moment, Jay didn't just get permission to keep creating—he got affirmation that his choices were valid, safe, and respected. Daniel got a new frame for understanding expression. And the rest of the class got a quiet lesson in freedom.

Jay's moment is proof: interrupting gender myths in real time is often less about a grand speech and more about an intentional, values-based choice.

Jay's experience shows how myths about "boy colors" and "girl materials" quietly police children's choices. Ms. Reyes's response shows how one moment can interrupt that myth and replace it with truth.

If myths tell us *what's false*, environments reveal *what's practiced.*

It's one thing to intellectually reject the idea that "gender is binary" or that "kids are too young to know who they are." It's another to examine whether our classrooms, hallways, libraries, and playgrounds actually reflect that truth. Every policy, poster, pronoun, and practice either reinforces restrictive norms or opens the door to affirmation.

Figure 2.3 offers real-world classroom scenarios to help us see how the same moment can either uphold the myths we've just dismantled or embody the truths we've committed to living out.

FIGURE 2.3
Moving from Restrictive to Affirming Classrooms

Scenario	Restrictive Environment	Affirming Environment
Morning Meeting Introductions	The teacher says, "Good morning, boys and girls," reinforcing binary gender categories and excluding nonbinary students.	The teacher says, "Good morning, scholars/friends/leaders," using inclusive, non-gendered greetings that affirm all identities.
Classroom Library	Books feature only cisgender, heterosexual characters and traditional gender roles.	The library includes diverse characters across the gender spectrum, with stories showing boys nurturing, girls leading, and nonbinary youth thriving.
Student Dress Choices	Students wearing clothing outside gender norms are told it's "not appropriate" or asked to change.	Student dress choices are respected as long as they meet general safety and comfort guidelines; individuality is celebrated.
Play and Activities	Blocks are given to boys and dolls are given to girls during free play.	All toys and activities are available to every student without gendered expectations.
Responding to Pronouns	The educator avoids using a student's pronouns or insists on "what's in the system."	The educator uses the student's self-identified name and pronouns consistently, correcting mistakes and modeling respect for others.

Jay's art project wasn't just about pink paper and glitter—it was a living test of the myths we've been unlearning. In that moment, Ms. Reyes didn't just correct a comment; she modeled a truth that rippled through her classroom: expression is for everyone.

The move may have felt small, but it's exactly how culture shifts—one choice at a time. Jay left that table knowing he was safe to show up fully as himself. Daniel left with a seed planted for a broader understanding of gender and expression. The rest of the class left with a living example of what affirmation looks and sounds like.

The bridge from this single moment to sustained cultural change lies in *intentional practice*:

- **Name the harm** when myths surface, without shaming the student who voiced them.
- **Model the truth** in your language and choices so students see it lived, not just stated.
- **Embed it in your systems**—classroom routines, materials, and curriculum—so it becomes the norm rather than the exception.

When we connect our myth-busting language to real-time action, we create learning spaces where identity isn't policed—it's celebrated. Jay's glitter card wasn't an isolated win; it was a starting point for a classroom that tells every student: *You belong here, exactly as you are.*

From Insight to Action: Everyday Moves That Shift Culture

Knowing the truth is a start. Living it in our practice is the real work. Every hallway interaction, read-aloud choice, field trip, and family email becomes an opportunity to either reinforce the myths or dismantle them.

Here are some strategies you can begin using tomorrow:

1. Make inclusion visible.
    - Display affirming symbols—rainbow stickers, pronoun badges, inclusive book covers—not as decoration but as an open invitation to safety.
    - Incorporate representation in all subjects, not just during Pride Month or special assemblies.
2. Speak with precision and care.
    - Use a student's self-identified name and pronouns consistently.
    - Replace gendered group calls like "boys and girls" with inclusive terms like "scholars," "team," or "friends."
3. Audit your curriculum and materials.
    - Review books, worksheets, and visuals for stereotypes or erasure.
    - Add resources that depict diverse gender identities, family structures, and cultural expressions as everyday, not exceptional.
4. Interrupt bias in real time.
    - If a student makes a hurtful comment, address it in the moment and explain why it's harmful.
    - Redirect language and actions without shaming while focusing on learning and accountability.
5. Partner with families and communities.
    - Invite parents, caregivers, and local advocates into conversations about gender inclusion.
    - Share resources proactively so they understand the "why" behind inclusive practices.

When we embed these moves into our daily rhythm, we shift from reactive allyship to proactive advocacy. Over time, our consistency becomes the loudest message: *In this space, your identity is not up for debate—it's a given.*

Language Is Liberation—But Only If We Use It

Here's the truth: words alone will not save our students—but they can absolutely harm them. The language we choose in our classrooms, emails, meetings, and curricula is the scaffolding that either holds our students up or boxes them in. And for queer and trans youth—especially those of color—language can be the first sign that a space is safe . . . or it isn't.

That's why this chapter is not just about knowing terms—it's about refusing to weaponize ignorance, even unintentionally. It's about naming myths before they calcify into policy. It's about replacing silence with clarity, euphemisms with truth, and assumptions with curiosity.

You don't have to overhaul every sentence overnight, but you do have to make the choice, every day, to align your language with your values.

Language is not neutral. It always points somewhere—toward belonging or erasure, toward liberation or compliance. And when we, as educators, choose affirming language, we are telling every queer and trans student: *You belong here, exactly as you are.*

This work asks us to move

- From avoiding the "hard" conversations to initiating them with care.
- From language as habit to language as intentional practice.
- From passive awareness to active interruption of harm.

No one becomes free through silence, not the 5th grader testing out new pronouns, not the high school senior who's never heard their identity named with respect, and not the educator who's been waiting for permission to speak truth in their own voice.

Whether you are a school leader crafting policy, a teacher choosing read-alouds, or a parent preparing your child for the first day of school—your language is part of the ecosystem our students will inherit. You don't have to be perfect to be BRAVE with your words—you just have to be intentional.

And when the work feels heavy, remember: every time you speak an affirming word, interrupt a stereotype, or replace a myth with truth, you are not just talking—you are building a world.

Key Takeaways

- Language shapes reality. Inclusive, precise, and affirming language communicates safety and belonging.
- Myths about gender and sexuality are not harmless misunderstandings—they cause real harm when left unchallenged.
- Educators must actively replace binary, stereotypical, or erasing language with terms that reflect the full spectrum of identity.
- Daily language choices—from greetings to feedback to curriculum—signal whether queer and trans youth are valued or erased.
- The BRAVE framework offers a lens for evaluating our language and ensuring it aligns with our commitment to belonging, respect, advocacy, visibility, and empathy.

BRAVE Reflection Questions

Before moving forward, take a moment to reflect using the BRAVE framework:

- **Belonging:** Does my language invite every student to feel at home in this space?
- **Respect:** Am I consistent in using names and pronouns as students request—especially when it's not convenient?
- **Advocacy:** Where am I willing to disrupt language that harms, even if it's subtle?
- **Visibility:** Does my spoken, written, and visual language reflect the presence of queer and trans people in our community?
- **Empathy:** How can my own story help me better understand the weight and meaning language holds for my students?

Chapter 2 Playlist

You've just explored a chapter that asks us to unlearn, relearn, and speak with intention. Now, visit www.ccmeducationgroup.co to take this work further with a curated collection of articles, research briefs, and educator tools that expand on the themes of language, myths, and action.

You'll find

- Glossaries and guides from leading LGBTQIA+ organizations.
- Research summaries on gender norms, stereotypes, and their impact in education.
- Classroom tools for practicing inclusive greetings, correcting missteps, and interrupting harm.
- Media and podcasts that model affirming language in storytelling and public discourse.

Use these resources to

- Lead a professional learning session with your team.
- Deepen your personal practice as an educator or leader.
- Facilitate a parent/community workshop on inclusive language.

PART II

THE BRAVE FRAMEWORK IN ACTION

3

Building True Belonging in Our Classrooms and Schools

"We deserve to experience love fully, equally, without shame and without compromise."
—Elliot Page

Belonging Isn't Just a Buzzword—It's the Foundation

Belonging is more than simply feeling welcome—it's the deep, unshakable knowing that you are accepted, valued, and essential to the life of a community. Psychologist Abraham Maslow placed belonging at the center of his Hierarchy of Needs, just after safety and physiological needs, recognizing it as a fundamental driver of human motivation and growth. Without belonging, higher-order learning, creativity, and self-actualization are nearly impossible.

In education, belonging has moved from being an abstract, feel-good idea to a measurable driver of academic engagement, mental health, and long-term student success. The American Public Health Association (2024) notes that belonging is particularly protective for LGBTQIA+ youth—serving as a buffer against discrimination, bias, and social isolation. Schools that intentionally build belonging see better attendance, stronger relationships, and reduced behavioral incidents, while those that fail to do so can unintentionally perpetuate harm and exclusion.

The origins of belonging as an educational construct are rooted in social psychology and community development theory. Early research emphasized "fitting in"—adapting to the dominant norms of a group—while more recent scholarship reframes belonging as being accepted as your authentic self (Aarons-Martin, 2023). This is a crucial shift for LGBTQIA+ students and other historically marginalized groups, because belonging is not about assimilation into dominant culture—it's about transforming environments so all identities are honored and affirmed.

In today's context, belonging in schools is both a cultural condition and a strategic priority. As Brown (2017) frames it, true belonging requires courage: it's the act of showing up as you are, and the collective work of ensuring every person can do the same without fear. In practice, that means leaders must move beyond surface-level inclusion to redesign policies, daily interactions, and the very fabric of school culture so that belonging is not the exception but the norm.

The principles of belonging take on their deepest meaning when we see them lived out in real classrooms, where theory meets the day-to-day realities of teaching. Research can tell us that belonging requires authenticity, safety, and systemic affirmation, but it is in the actions of educators that these ideas gain power. At Lincoln Harvard Elementary School, one teacher—Mr. Morales—embodies this truth, as you'll see in the next section. His classroom is not just a site of learning but a sanctuary where students, especially those whose identities challenge dominant norms, see that liberation is possible. Through his story, we witness how belonging in schools is not simply about fitting in—it is about transforming the environment so that every student, and every educator, can show up fully as themselves.

Introducing Mr. Morales and the Unapologetic Classroom

Belonging in schools does not live in mission statements—it lives in people. Mr. Morales is one of those people. At Lincoln Harvard Elementary, he embodies the kind of leadership that Chapter 1 and Chapter 2 challenge us to envision: leadership that is both structurally aware and unapologetically human. As one of the rare Afro-Latine teachers—part of the mere 1.3 percent of Black men in the teaching workforce (Heubeck, 2025)—he is a living counter-narrative to the invisibility many students experience.

Mr. Morales infuses his classroom with cultural pride, high expectations, and a curriculum rooted in justice and joy. Students rap the water cycle, celebrate Afro-Latine artists, and write poems about identity and freedom. Yet, outside his room, he navigates coded critiques, sidelong glances at his painted nails, and "helpful" suggestions to stick to the "standard" curriculum. The subtext is always the same: *You don't fit the mold.*

His response is steady: "Belonging isn't a bonus—it's the baseline."

Every day, Mr. Morales walks the tightrope between brilliance and backlash. His visibility as a gender-expressive, justice-driven educator makes him a target for subtle and overt pushback—but also a beacon for students who have never before seen their whole selves reflected in a teacher. His classroom is a sanctuary, not because of décor or slogans but because it operates on the radical premise that authenticity is nonnegotiable. When a child who has never felt seen before finally experiences recognition in Mr. Morales's room, it plants the seed of possibility.

But belonging is never just about one teacher—it's about the systems that sustain or sabotage it. And in the same hallways where Mr. Morales offers sanctuary, other students' stories reveal just how fragile belonging can be when it depends on individual champions rather than institutional commitment.

Reagan's Story: Belonging as Lifeline

In Mr. Morales's 4th grade class sits Reagan—a vibrant and resilient student navigating the complex landscape of school life with a unique blend of courage and vulnerability. As a queer, gender-nonconforming child of biracial heritage, Reagan's journey is shaped by the search for identity and acceptance in the predominantly white and conservative environment of their new school in Bolton, Massachusetts.

Outside the classroom, Reagan channels their energy into music and skateboarding, finding both solace and connection in these passions. But within the walls of school, the weight of misgendering, harassment, and invisibility is constant. Roll call becomes a daily trial, with teachers stumbling over pronouns—some correcting awkwardly, others ignoring them altogether. In hallways, Reagan absorbs cruel taunts: "What are you today, Reagan?" or "Can't decide if you're more white or Black . . . or a boy or a girl?"

Even in group projects, their contributions are questioned: "Why should we listen to you? You're not even sure who you are." Sometimes, the harm comes from adults cloaked in good intentions. A teacher once advised, "Maybe if you dressed more like the other boys or girls, you'd fit in better." These micro- and macroaggressions accumulate into a heavy truth Reagan once shared with a counselor: "It's like I'm invisible. They see right through me—or worse, they wish they could."

In most classrooms, Reagan's existence is barely acknowledged. The curriculum offers no mirrors, only windows into dominant narratives. Questions about absent LGBTQIA+ histories are met with "We have to stick to the curriculum." Even so-called "safe" spaces feel shallow—with counselors offering platitudes like "Just be yourself, and people will come around" without grasping the daily courage that requires.

But in Mr. Morales's class, the air shifts. His room is a place where Reagan's pronouns are honored without hesitation, their music celebrated as genius, their skateboard tricks recognized as art. It's where they are not reduced to their difference but expanded by their brilliance. For Reagan, Mr. Morales is not just a teacher—he's proof that visibility and belonging can exist in the same space.

Belonging by Design: What the Data Demand

Brené Brown (2017) reminds us that "true belonging doesn't require you to change who you are; it requires you to be who you are." Yet too often, schools confuse belonging with fitting in—rewarding students and teachers for assimilation rather than honoring their differences. For LGBTQIA+ youth, particularly those who are Black, Latine, Indigenous, or Asian, this confusion isn't benign; it's dangerous.

Research underscores what students have been saying for decades. Patricia Moran's (2023) literature review at Lesley University calls belonging "a critical protective factor for LGBTQ youth," especially when it is nurtured through arts, storytelling, and community spaces that affirm identity. Conversely, trans youth advocate Kiran Yeh (2023) warns that when adults avoid conversations about gender identity—or claim they "don't understand"—they send a clear message of exclusion. Silence, in these cases, isn't neutral; it erases.

This erasure shows up in small but powerful ways:

- The pause before saying a student's name
- Intake forms without inclusive options
- Hallway slurs met with silence rather than action

And belonging shows up just as clearly:

- Being greeted by name and affirmed pronouns
- Seeing yourself reflected in books, posters, and lessons
- Knowing your dignity will be defended
- Accessing bathrooms, sports teams, or clubs without debate about your identity

Belonging is never a hallway poster or a one-off diversity week event. It's the result of hundreds of intentional actions embedded into curriculum, policy, and daily culture.

Mr. Morales lives this truth. He designs a classroom where justice and joy are foundational. His classroom hums with cultural pride and high expectations.

Outside his door, however, the climate shifts. "Your approach is . . . unconventional," a colleague offered once, tiptoeing around their discomfort.

Others whisper about his appearance: "Did you see the nail polish he had on today? A bit much for a teacher, don't you think?"

Even at a parent–teacher conference, one parent said after a lesson on the history of the Stonewall riots, "We appreciate your enthusiasm, but maybe stick to the standard curriculum." Translation: *You're making us uncomfortable.*

These moments aren't isolated—they reflect national trends. A 2024 American Public Health Association report found that 69 percent of LGBTQIA+ students experience discrimination at school, with curriculum exclusion among the most common forms. Educators who affirm queer identities often face professional isolation, backlash from peers and parents, and pressure to self-censor—factors that contribute to burnout and drive many out of the profession altogether (Pinckney, 2021).

Mr. Morales refuses to shrink. "Our children deserve to see the diverse world they're a part of," he says. "Belonging isn't a bonus—it's the foundation of all that matters here." Yet maintaining that foundation means walking a daily tightrope between brilliance and backlash, where every lesson, outfit choice, and word carries risk.

For students like Reagan, that risk is survival. Research (Fukuda et al., 2024) documents the toll of a steady drip of microaggressions: these daily invalidations compound into measurable harm, driving higher rates of anxiety, depression, and disengagement among LGBTQIA+ youth of color.

In most spaces, Reagan is told—implicitly or explicitly—that fitting in means erasing themselves. But in Mr. Morales's class, the rules change. Pronouns are respected without hesitation. Their music and skateboarding skills are celebrated as integral to who they are. They see themselves in the posters, the history lessons, and the stories read aloud.

The Pinckney (2021) study on culturally responsive pedagogy confirms what Reagan feels: when students see their identities affirmed in curriculum and practice, they report stronger senses of belonging, academic motivation, and emotional safety. For Mr. Morales, affirmation isn't an extra—it's infrastructure.

"They say my nail polish is unprofessional, but I see it as a conversation starter about self-expression and respect," he says. "If one student feels more comfortable being themselves because they saw me being me, then it's worth it."

Reagan is that "one student" who sees Mr. Morales stand unapologetically in his truth as a quiet lifeline—living proof that authenticity and belonging are possible, even in a world determined to make them impossible.

Building Belonging at Every Level: Practical Tools for Classrooms, Teams, and Schools

Why Belonging Matters

Reagan's time in Mr. Morales's class shows us something important: belonging doesn't just happen. It's something we build, protect, and keep alive. A single teacher's encouragement can make a student feel seen, but if the school around them stays the same, that sense of safety can disappear as soon as they step out the door.

Belonging isn't just a nice idea—it's essential for learning and for life. For many LGBTQIA+ students and educators, being themselves can still feel unsafe. Rules, lessons, and even the silence of adults can send the message that it's safer to hide who you are.

From Story to Action

Belonging doesn't grow by accident. It takes intentional, everyday actions that ripple outward—from individual classrooms to entire school systems. That's why the next set of tools is organized into practical tiers. Each figure offers a different entry point for teachers looking to change daily routines, for teams ready to shift staff culture, and for leaders seeking to redesign policies and systems. Together, they help every educator see where to start, where to grow, and how to sustain belonging so students like Reagan—and the adults who serve them—can thrive.

How to Use the Figures in This Section

Figures 3.1 through 3.4 are designed as a complete toolkit for building belonging across classrooms, teams, and entire school communities:

- Start with Figure 3.1 to choose practical, tiered strategies for creating inclusive environments for students.
- Use Figure 3.2 as a self-assessment to reflect on your own daily practices, set growth goals, and track progress over time.
- Move to Figure 3.3 to extend belonging beyond the classroom—into staff culture, family engagement, and partnerships—so every adult connected to your school experiences the same respect and affirmation you want for students.
- Invite students to use Figure 3.4 for their own self-reflection, helping them become active co-creators of welcoming spaces.

Taken together, these tools support individual growth, team collaboration, and systemwide transformation.

A Tiered Approach to Belonging

Belonging doesn't stop with kind words or inclusive posters. To move beyond surface-level gestures toward real, lasting inclusion, we need action at every level—not just in individual classrooms but also across schools and districts.

That's why this framework uses three tiers:

- Tier 1 includes everyday practices for all classrooms and communities—shifts in language, routines, and group norms.
- Tier 2 focuses on targeted support for LGBTQIA+ students navigating misgendering, invisibility, and other harms.
- Tier 3 addresses big-picture systems—policies, structures, and visuals—that can either create or block belonging.

Educators can use this framework to see where they are now, choose their next steps, and work with students to create more welcoming spaces. School and district leaders can fold these practices into staff training, policy reviews, and community events.

When belonging is woven into every level of a school—not just in the hearts of a few caring teachers—we go beyond "safe" spaces and create places where students can truly thrive.

The following pages provide ready-to-use strategies drawn from research, real classrooms, and the experiences of educators like Mr. Morales. Each tier includes examples, sample scripts, and leadership tips to help every student feel not only safe but also seen, valued, and celebrated.

Building Belonging in Action

Belonging is built through small daily habits, intentional responses, and systemwide change. Figure 3.1 offers a tiered framework you can adapt to your classroom, program, or district. Each tier builds on the last:

- **Tier 1: Universal practices** are for all students, in all spaces. They shape everyday language, routines, and group norms so every student hears *You belong here without exception.* Examples include using inclusive greetings, inviting (but not requiring) pronoun sharing, and incorporating identity-affirming visuals into the classroom. Leaders can embed these practices into staff meetings, newsletters, and onboarding to normalize them across the school.

- **Tier 2: Targeted practices** focus on students who may face misgendering, invisibility, or bias. They involve intentional check-ins, quiet acts of allyship, and visible cues of safety—like a Safe Space sticker or the transgender pride flag. Leaders can support these efforts through coaching, resource updates, and data reviews to address gaps in support and discipline outcomes.
- **Tier 3: Intensive practices** address the structures and policies that either uphold or dismantle belonging. This includes creating accessible gender-neutral restrooms, updating exclusionary traditions, and using restorative circles in place of punitive discipline. Leaders at this level commit to ongoing equity audits, funding LGBTQIA+ student programs, and prioritizing diverse hiring pipelines.

FIGURE 3.1

Tiered Strategies to Build Belonging in Schools

Tier	Focus Area	Practice/Strategy	Example Script or Action
1. Universal Practices	Inclusive Language	Use affirming greetings and titles.	"Good morning, leaders. I'm Mr. Morales, and I use he/him pronouns."
	Group Identity Cues	Replace gendered terms with inclusive labels.	"Writers, please bring your notebooks." "Mathematicians, let's problem solve together."
	Normalizing Expression	Affirm personal choices in dress, colors, or hobbies.	"Thanks for sharing. Nail polish isn't just for one gender—it's about how we express ourselves."
2. Targeted Practices	Pronoun Respect	Correct misgendering with care.	"Actually, Jay uses he/him pronouns. Thanks for adjusting."
	Private Check-Ins	Follow up when harm may have occurred.	"Hey, I noticed today seemed tough. Anything I can do to make this space feel better for you?"
	Allyship Moments	Co-create scripts with students for responding to bias.	"Let's practice what you'd want to say. I'll stand by you however you need."
3. Intensive Practices	Visual Cues and Symbols	Display pride flags, inclusive signage, and safe-space markers.	Hang the Progress Pride flag. Include posters of LGBTQIA+ leaders and affirming messages.
	Policy and Environment	Review dress codes, bathroom access, and curricula for bias.	Update policies to allow gender-neutral dress. Normalize access to all-gender bathrooms.
	Restorative Culture	Facilitate healing when harm happens.	"Let's talk about how that comment landed. We repair here—we don't ignore harm."

Whether you're a classroom teacher, program director, or district leader, this framework serves as both a self-assessment tool and a roadmap. Start where you are, build momentum, and work in partnership with students, families, and colleagues. The goal isn't just safety—it's to create environments where every student feels seen, valued, and celebrated.

Self-Assessment for Belonging Practices

Use Figure 3.2 to reflect on how consistently you integrate belonging practices into your daily work. This isn't about perfection—it's about awareness and growth. Mark the box that best reflects your current practice, and then choose one or two areas to strengthen over the next month.

- Complete this self-assessment and then revisit it quarterly to track growth.
- Use your results to select one or two practices to strengthen before adding more.
- School leaders can adapt this as part of classroom observations, coaching cycles, or PD follow-ups to support sustained change.

FIGURE 3.2
Belonging Practices Self-Assessment

Practice	Always	Sometimes	Not Yet
I invite pronouns during introductions and model my own.			
I use gender-neutral language when addressing groups.			
I correct misgendering in real time with care and respect.			
I check in privately with students who may be struggling.			
I display Safe Space symbols, pride flags, or affirming visuals.			
I advocate for inclusive policies in staff meetings or leadership spaces.			
I include LGBTQIA+ topics, figures, or history in lessons, activities, or bulletin boards.			

Tiered Strategies for Community Support

Belonging doesn't stop at the classroom door. These strategies help staff and leaders foster affirming, respectful relationships with LGBTQIA+ adults in the school community—whether they're colleagues, caregivers, or partner organizations.

- Leaders can integrate these into onboarding, staff handbooks, and partnership agreements.
- Use the tiers to plan professional learning for staff and volunteers.
- Pair this table with Figure 3.2 to ensure both student and adult belonging are addressed in your culture work.

FIGURE 3.3
Tiered Strategies for Supporting LGBTQIA+ Adults in Our Community

Tier	Focus Area	Practice/Strategy	Example Script or Action
1. Universal	Inclusive Language	Use affirming names, pronouns, and titles in meetings, emails, and introductions.	"This is Jordan Rivera, our new family liaison. Jordan uses they/them pronouns."
	Visible Welcome	Display inclusive symbols and materials in staff areas, family spaces, and public communications.	Add pride or Progress Pride symbols to event flyers and welcome packets.
	Neutral Event Planning	Design events and communications to be inclusive of all family structures and identities.	Replace "Moms' Night" with "Family Night" or "Caregiver Meet-Up."
2. Targeted	Allyship in Action	Address bias or exclusion when it occurs, whether in staff rooms or community spaces.	"I just want to pause; that comment could be harmful. Let's reframe it."
	Intentional Check-Ins	Offer private support to colleagues, partners, or caregivers after difficult incidents.	"I noticed that the meeting got tense. Do you want to talk or need me to step in next time?"
	Representation in Roles	Invite LGBTQIA+ voices into planning committees, advisory councils, and leadership positions.	Proactively ask LGBTQIA+ parents to co-lead a family engagement event.
3. Intensive	Policy and Structure	Review and update policies to protect LGBTQIA+ adults from discrimination in employment, partnerships, and participation.	Include sexual orientation and gender identity in nondiscrimination clauses.
	Training and Accountability	Provide ongoing PD for staff, volunteers, and partners on inclusive language, bias interruption, and cultural responsiveness.	Schedule annual "Belonging for All" training with LGBTQIA+ facilitators.
	Crisis and Harm Response	Use restorative practices to address harm and rebuild trust when incidents occur.	Facilitate a mediated conversation between staff and caregiver after a harmful exchange.

Get Students Involved

Belonging isn't just the job of adults—it's a shared responsibility that includes the voices, choices, and leadership of young people. When students have the tools and space to reflect on their own experiences, they become powerful co-creators of inclusive, affirming school communities.

The self-assessment in Figure 3.4 invites students to pause and consider: *What does belonging look and feel like in my classroom, my school, and among my peers?* This tool helps young people name what's working, what's missing, and how they might contribute to a stronger sense of community for themselves and others.

Educators can use this checklist during

- Morning meetings or advisory sessions.
- Restorative circles or community-building days.
- One-on-one conversations with trusted adults (counselors, mentors, or teachers).
- Youth leadership, GSA, or peer mentoring programs.

Invite students to use it for private reflection or group dialogue. When students feel empowered to reflect and speak up, they shift from passive participants to active agents of change.

FIGURE 3.4

I Create Belonging Too: Student Self-Assessment

Belonging Practice	Yes	Sometimes	Not Yet
I feel safe to be myself at school.			
I see books, posters, or lessons that include people like me or my family.			
My teachers or leaders use my name and pronouns correctly.			
I feel like my culture, identity, or story is respected.			
I can name at least one adult at school I trust or can talk to if something is wrong.			
I know where to go or who to talk to if I feel left out, bullied, or unsafe.			
I've been invited to share my ideas or stories in class, a club, or a project.			
I've been part of helping others feel welcome, even if they are different from me.			

Belonging Is Not an Accident—It's an Intention

Here's the truth: inclusion is not belonging. Inclusion says, "You can be here." Belonging says, "This space was built with you in mind." And for queer and trans youth—especially those of color—belonging is often the difference between surviving the day and daring to thrive.

That's why this chapter is not just about seating charts, bulletin boards, or advisory activities—it's about designing communities where no one has to wonder if they matter. It's about shifting from compliance to connection, from token gestures to a living culture that says, "We see you. We need you. You belong here."

Being BRAVE with belonging might look like

- Greeting every student by name and pronoun before the lesson begins.
- Inviting a student to co-lead a community circle—even if they've never spoken in front of peers before.
- Replacing "fit in" norms with rituals that celebrate difference and individuality.
- Using your influence in a staff meeting to advocate for policy changes that protect LGBTQIA+ youth.
- Making sure school hallways, curriculum, and assemblies reflect the diversity of your actual student body—not just the dominant narrative.

You don't have to dismantle every barrier in one day—but you do have to choose, every day, to create conditions where all students can see themselves reflected and respected.

Belonging is not neutral. It either roots us in community or pushes us to the margins. And when we, as educators, choose to build belonging intentionally, we tell every student, "You were never an afterthought. This space was made for you."

This work asks us to move

- From assuming "everyone feels welcome" to actively checking in on who still feels unseen.

- From symbolic gestures to sustained practices that foster trust and safety.
- From one-size-fits-all programs to layered, culturally responsive strategies that honor the complexity of identity.

No one experiences true belonging through silence or assumption—not the student who's the only one of their identity in the room, not the teacher afraid to be out at work, not the parent wondering if they're safe to attend the school potluck.

Whether you are a school leader shaping policy, a teacher running morning meeting, or a community partner co-creating programming—your presence, choices, and advocacy form the ecosystem our students will inherit. You don't have to be perfect to be BRAVE with belonging; you just have to be intentional.

And when the work feels heavy, remember: every time you greet a student by name, invite them into leadership or reimagine a policy to affirm who they are. You are not just running a classroom—you are building a world.

Key Takeaways

- Inclusion is not belonging. Inclusion says, "You can be here." Belonging says, "This space was built with you in mind."
- Belonging must be intentionally designed—through visuals, rituals, language, policies, and relationships that affirm students of all identities and abilities.
- One adult can change everything. When students feel seen, protected, and like coauthors of classroom culture, they thrive.
- Belonging is disrupted when educators rely on assumptions, silence, or control-based norms—especially for queer, trans, neurodivergent, and BIPOC (Black, Indigenous, people of color) youth.
- True belonging draws on cultural wisdom. When we embrace communal, ancestral practices—like storytelling, shared leadership, and circle processes—we undo the isolation embedded in traditional schooling.

BRAVE Reflection Questions

Before moving forward, take a moment to reflect using the BRAVE framework:

- **Belonging:** What does belonging feel like in your school or organization—and who might still be waiting for an invitation to be fully themselves?
- **Respect:** How do you respond when students or staff express identities that challenge traditional expectations—and how might you build respectful habits that affirm difference?
- **Advocacy:** Where are your policies, practices, or traditions excluding LGBTQIA+ voices—and how can you advocate for those being left out?
- **Visibility:** What signals do your hallways, lesson plans, or staff meetings send about who belongs—and who doesn't?
- **Empathy:** When you think back to your own youth, who helped you feel like you mattered—and how can you be that person for someone else today?

Chapter 3 Playlist

You've just explored a chapter that calls you to reimagine belonging as both a daily practice and a shared responsibility. Now, take this work further. Visit www.ccmeducationgroup.co to access a curated set of resources to deepen your practice and activate belonging in your setting:

- Research on belonging and mental health.
- Inclusive classroom tools and checklists.
- Brave student and educator storytelling podcasts.
- Equity-centered policy templates.
- Schoolwide activities that honor queer and trans identities.

Use these resources to

- Lead a professional learning session with your team.
- Facilitate a family engagement night on building belonging.
- Conduct a schoolwide belonging audit with staff and students.

4

Respect Is a Two-Way Street

"My identity is not up for debate. You don't have to understand me to respect me."

—Alok Vaid-Menon

Respect Without Reciprocity: Lessons from a Detention Turned Classroom

It was supposed to be a consequence. But it became a classroom.

One Tuesday afternoon, I sat with four 8th graders in after-school detention. They were all serving time for being disruptive in their math class—one led by a cis-het male teacher known for his strict tone and tight boundaries.

The students—Tânia, Catarina, Sofía, and Malik—were each 13 years old. Tânia and Catarina, Cape Verdean girls, often moved as a unit, bold in their brilliance and protective of each other. Sofía, a Dominican and Puerto Rican student, had a dry wit and a low tolerance for injustice. Malik, biracial (Black and white), wore his emotions close to the surface, often acting out what he didn't yet have the words to express.

What started as a gripe session about "unfair punishment" quickly turned into something deeper.

Catarina spoke first: "You know Mr. D called Ray the wrong name again, right? We already told him Ray goes by he/him now."

Malik added, "He laughed. Thought it was a joke. Said something like, 'That's what y'all are going with today?'"

Sofía rolled her eyes. "Ray got mad. Started cussing him out. And Mr. D got all loud like he was the victim."

I listened.

Then Tânia said what I couldn't stop thinking about later: "Respect goes both ways. If teachers want it, they've gotta show it—especially when we've already told them something important."

The room got quiet. And then, like a floodgate had opened, the conversation spilled into everything—dating, identity, pressure, consent, labels, confusion, and safety. Two of the girls shared that they were questioning their sexuality and weren't sure how to talk to anyone about liking other girls. Sofía admitted she'd heard teachers at lunch joking about "teen drama" when two boys held hands in the hallway. Malik said he didn't get why everyone at school acted like being straight was the default: "It's like . . . if you're not, you gotta explain yourself. Over and over."

They weren't asking for special treatment. They were asking for safety, for teachers who didn't smirk when they mentioned a crush or act awkward when someone said they weren't straight or shut down conversations about consent and relationships because they felt "too adult."

What made them feel safe talking to me?

"You told us about your husband." Malik shrugged. "And you have that flag in your office. You're just . . . real."

In that moment, I was reminded that respect isn't just a value. It's a practice. It starts with visibility, continues with consistency, and grows through relationships.

Bridging the Story to Systemic Truths

When Ray and his classmates named the harm they experienced—and the inconsistencies in how adults wielded respect—it wasn't just a critique of a math teacher. It was a mirror held up to the entire system.

Their story reflects what too many queer and questioning youth of color encounter in schools: cultures that claim inclusion but are built on norms, policies, and hierarchies that perpetuate exclusion. These students weren't being "difficult" or "disrespectful." They were naming a deep truth: the rules we create in schools often contradict the very respect we demand from students.

And that contradiction isn't accidental. It is rooted in a larger architecture—a set of deeply embedded values aligned with what scholars describe as white supremacist culture. These values shape how we define "appropriate" behavior, how we enforce rules, and how we respond to differences. They surface when we expect compliance without question, prioritize comfort over conflict, and mistake silence for safety (Padayachee & Kriger, 2024).

For neurodivergent students, respect is often denied because their communication or coping strategies fall outside what schools deem "appropriate." Whether it's scripting, stimming, or needing more processing time, neurodivergent ways of being are too often treated as disruptions instead of differences. When these students are also queer, trans, or BIPOC, the pathologizing—and the policing—intensifies. This isn't simply about classroom management; it's about safety, dignity, and the right to exist without being forced to conform.

Here's the truth: these values are not universal, not neutral, and certainly not "just good teaching." They are products of colonial legacies of control, discipline, and hierarchy (Padayachee & Kriger, 2024; Ladson-Billings, 1995). And they too often erase the wisdom, fluidity, and relationality found in BIPOC cultures and ancestral practices of care.

Why It Matters

Respect is culturally and historically constructed. In schools, "respect" often reflects white, cis-heteronormative, neurotypical, and middle-class norms. Without unpacking that, well-meaning educators may believe they are being respectful while actually enforcing assimilation (Ladson-Billings, 1995).

Respect is relational, not conditional. For LGBTQIA+ youth—especially those who are BIPOC—respect means having their identity affirmed and defended even when adults do not fully understand it. It is not earned by behavior; it is extended as a baseline human right (Pinckney, 2021).

Respect is a safety practice. It is not just politeness; it is a proactive stance that reduces harm. Research consistently links perceived respect from teachers to increased belonging, attendance, and academic engagement for LGBTQIA+ youth (Pinckney, 2021).

The Hidden Curriculum of Control

Research by Love (2019), Marrun (2022), and Pinckney (2021) challenges the default frameworks that shape classroom management and school norms. These studies show how traditional models—like "no talking," "track the speaker," or "sit up straight"—don't just create order; they erase cultural ways of being and police bodies that fall outside of white, cisgender, neurotypical, and heteronormative norms.

Ray wasn't punished for "disruption" alone. He was punished for existing outside a binary system that could not accommodate them. In this way, queer and trans youth of color often become the targets of what Damien Sojoyner (2013) calls the *carceral logic* of schooling—a system that disciplines, isolates, and punishes difference under the guise of order.

What's Often Left Out of the Conversation

What rarely enters the room—especially when we set classroom rules and rituals—are the ancestral models of community building that many BIPOC cultures have practiced for generations:

- In many Indigenous communities, talking circles are sacred spaces for shared voice and deep listening—long before Western restorative justice gave it a name.
- In Black and Afro-Caribbean traditions, call-and-response, rhythm, storytelling, and collective expression are ways of teaching and healing—not distractions.
- In Filipinx cultures, *kapwa* (shared inner self) emphasizes deep relationality and empathy as the foundation for interaction and belonging.
- In Latine communities, *familismo* holds space for intergenerational wisdom, mutual care, and accountability through collective decision making.

These frameworks center interdependence over individualism, community over compliance, and presence over perfection. When respected and reclaimed, they offer liberatory alternatives to the rigid systems that currently define—and often distort—respect in schools.

Centering Trans and Two-Spirit Wisdom

Decolonial educators remind us that gender fluidity, queerness, and transness are not modern inventions—they are Indigenous, global, and ancestral. Across many cultures, including those of Turtle Island, the Philippines, and the Pacific Islands, queer and trans people held honored, sacred roles long before colonization imposed binary, Christian, Eurocentric gender constructs. From a decolonizing classroom management perspective, examining the cultural assumptions and norms that shape "acceptable" behavior is essential to dismantling practices that marginalize queer and trans youth of color.

Culturally relevant pedagogy, as articulated by Ladson-Billings (1995), challenges dominant definitions of "respect" and "good teaching" that often privilege white, cisgender, neurotypical, and middle-class norms. Instead, it calls for three interdependent pillars: (1) academic success, (2) cultural competence, and (3) critical consciousness—the capacity for students to analyze and challenge societal inequities. When applied to LGBTQIA+ youth, particularly those from BIPOC and neurodivergent communities, respect must reflect this deeper, relational, and emancipatory vision rather than a compliance-based one.

Affirming these identities is not simply a modern DEI checkbox; it is a restorative return to ways of being where identity, connection, and liberation are inseparable. As Pinckney (2021) notes in *Intersecting Spaces: A Narrative Inquiry of Queer, Black, Indigenous, People of Color in Higher Education*, affirming LGBTQIA+ students through culturally responsive pedagogy strengthens their sense of belonging, academic motivation, and emotional safety. If our classroom norms ignore these frameworks—and instead prioritize rigidity, control, and shame—we do more than alienate students like Ray. We sever our connection to the very roots of liberatory education.

The contradictions Ray's classmates named do not disappear in younger grades; they simply take subtler forms. In 4th grade, they might emerge as lingering side-eyes, curriculum omissions, or staff who have not been taught to recognize what's missing. For students like Reagan, this invisibility can be just as isolating—and just as harmful—as overt acts of disrespect.

Reagan: 4th Grader, Musician, and Seeker of Belonging

Reagan is a vibrant, introspective 4th grade student with a sharp sense of humor, a deep love of music, and a talent for skateboarding that rivals kids twice their age. They are biracial—Black and white—and recently moved to Bolton, Massachusetts, from a more racially and culturally diverse city. The transition into this predominantly white, suburban school has felt like entering an entirely different world—one where the cues for safety, connection, and affirmation are far harder to detect.

Reagan identifies as queer and gender-nonconforming. They've always known they didn't fit neatly into the boxes others tried to place them in—whether related to gender, identity, or expression. At home, Reagan is surrounded by love: their parents, both artists, have affirmed their journey from the very beginning, encouraging self-expression and truth telling. But in school, Reagan often feels like a question mark in a world full of exclamation points. From the clothes they wear, to the way they speak, to the name they choose to go by, their mere presence often draws stares or whispered commentary.

In the classroom, Reagan is quick to raise their hand and passionate about reading and history. But they have learned to shrink themselves in response to the accumulation of microaggressions. Some are overt—like classmates making jokes about whether Reagan is a boy or a girl. Others are more insidious: teachers who misgender them and never correct themselves, group activities where peers exclude them with eye rolls or comments like "You're weird" or "You don't even know who you are." These daily indignities aren't always loud, but they're heavy.

Despite these challenges, Reagan is not just surviving—they are searching. They seek community, voice, and recognition. They wear a rainbow enamel pin on their backpack, not to make a statement but as a quiet signal to others who might understand. Music is their therapy; the gentle strum of their ukulele or the rhythm of their favorite beats often grounds them after a difficult day. They carry a notebook filled with songs, drawings, and affirmations written in gel pen. In the margins, they scribble lines like "Be who you needed when you were younger."

Reagan isn't just trying to exist in school—they're trying to matter.

Mr. Morales's Decolonized Restorative Approach: Listening First

Mr. Morales, an Afro-Latine 4th grade teacher known for his Afrobeat playlists, carefully curated classroom library, and intentional community-building rituals, had heard quiet rumblings about Reagan's experiences from colleagues. But it wasn't until a particularly painful moment—when Reagan was mocked during music class and left the room without explanation—that he knew it was time to do more than just check in.

He invited Reagan to join him during lunch the next day. No pressure—just one on one.

Reagan arrived holding their notebook like a shield. They slouched into the beanbag by Mr. Morales's window, the one with hanging plants and LGBTQIA+ affirming posters. It was quiet except for the soft hum of lo-fi beats and the occasional creak of the heater. Mr. Morales sat on a nearby stool—not behind his desk, not in front of the whiteboard, but at eye level.

Mr. Morales: "Thanks for coming, Reagan. You're not in trouble. I just want to check in. I've noticed some things—and I imagine you have too. But first, how's your heart today?"

Reagan (softly): "Tired, I guess. Tired of . . . existing."

Mr. Morales: "That's real. And I want you to know your existence is not just tolerated here—it's needed. But I have a feeling we haven't made that clear enough yet. Want to tell me what's been weighing on you?"

Reagan: "People stare. Like, all the time. Even teachers. And when they mess up my pronouns, it's like it doesn't even matter to them. Or they laugh, or say, 'It's hard to remember.' But I remember how to be polite to them."

Mr. Morales: "Whew . . . that hit me. I hear you. And I need to apologize—for the times I've made mistakes or stayed quiet when others did. That's not on you. That's on us."

There was a long silence. Mr. Morales didn't fill it.

Reagan: "I used to love school. I used to answer questions all the time. Now I just kind of float through the day hoping no one notices me too much."

Mr. Morales: "Floating takes strength when the current is working against you. But I don't want you to have to float. I want us to build something different, together."

Reagan: "How?"

Mr. Morales: "We start by listening. Then we change what needs changing—how we talk, how we teach, and how we name things in this classroom. Would you help me think through how this space can feel safer—not just for you but for anyone who feels like they're on the outside?"

Reagan: "Yeah. If it could help someone else . . . yeah."

From there, they co-designed new classroom norms around respect and identity, creating a Community Agreement Wall with language from Reagan's own reflections: "We listen to understand, not to correct" and "We all deserve to be seen, named, and honored."

Mr. Morales expanded the classroom library to include more queer, trans, and gender-expansive narratives, led morning meetings with prompts like "What helps you feel seen today?" and challenged colleagues during planning meetings when they defaulted to gendered assumptions. When Reagan faced another round of hallway teasing, Mr. Morales facilitated a circle—not just to repair harm but to center Reagan's voice and foster peer accountability.

"Restorative justice," he later told colleagues, "isn't just about fixing what's broken. It's about building what never existed in the first place—trust, equity, and a culture that doesn't make students like Reagan carry the burden of our silence."

His practices drew on decolonizing principles (Padayachee & Kriger, 2024), culturally relevant pedagogy (Ladson-Billings, 1995), and research on queer and trans students of color in educational spaces (Pinckney, 2021). He replaced punitive discipline with community-driven approaches rooted in ancestral traditions such as Ubuntu and Latine *consejos*—reminding his class often that "We are because we belong to each other."

Weeks later, Reagan's notebook held a new line: "I still get scared sometimes. But now I know at least one person sees me. And that makes school feel like mine too."

Why This Matters

Mr. Morales's approach disrupts the belief that discipline must be reactive, policy-driven, and hierarchical. Traditional models often ignore ancestral practices of healing and accountability in favor of rigid structures that erase cultural and gender diversity (Padayachee & Kriger, 2024).

In contrast, Morales's model—rooted in Two-Spirit and Indigenous frameworks, culturally relevant pedagogy, and racial justice-informed trans pedagogy—creates the conditions for real belonging (Ladson-Billings, 1995; Pinckney, 2021). Reagan was no longer invisible. They were an active participant in a community that honored their voice, identity, and humanity.

Respect in Action: Five Practices You Can Start Tomorrow

The stories of Jay and Reagan show that respect for LGBTQIA+ youth—especially those who are BIPOC and/or neurodivergent—is not abstract. It is the daily work of rethinking language, norms, and policies so students experience belonging in tangible ways. The following practices move respect from intention to action:

1. Lead with names and pronouns.
   - Model correct pronoun use in front of students, even when the student is not in the room (Human Rights Campaign, 2024b).
   - Normalize introductions that invite but don't require sharing pronouns.
   - Correct misgendering immediately and matter-of-factly: "Actually, he uses he/him," and continue without over-explaining or making it a spectacle.
2. Audit for representation.
   - Review classroom libraries, displays, and lesson examples for authentic representation of queer, trans, BIPOC, and neurodivergent identities.
   - Remove outdated or stereotyped portrayals. Incorporate titles and resources from queer and trans authors of color (Bigelow, 2022).
3. Co-create and revisit community agreements.
   - Develop classroom norms collaboratively, centering students most likely to be marginalized.
   - Include explicit language about respecting pronouns, challenging bias, and addressing harm (Human Rights Campaign, 2024b).
   - Revisit your norms, ethos, or agreements regularly—especially after harm occurs—to ensure they are living documents, not posters on the wall.

4. Interrupt disrespect in real time.
    - Address identity-based jokes, microaggressions, and side comments consistently.
    - Use restorative questions such as "What impact do you think those words had?" rather than relying only on punitive responses (Padayachee & Kriger, 2024).
5. Push for institutional commitments.
    - Advocate for gender-inclusive forms, name/pronoun updates in school databases, and pronoun affirmation training for all staff (Pinckney, 2021).
    - Support the adoption of anti-bias policies with clear accountability processes for reporting and addressing identity-based harm.

The Intersectionality of Respect

Respect is not experienced the same way by all LGBTQIA+ students. When race, disability, class, and other identity markers intersect, the stakes for respect are amplified. Research on queer, trans, and Two-Spirit students of color in Turtle Island and the Philippines underscores how overlapping systems of oppression compound microaggressions and increase vulnerability to punitive discipline (Mendoza & Johnson, 2024).

For example, a queer, neurodivergent Black student may experience

- Misgendering from teachers.
- Racialized discipline practices.
- Ableist assumptions about behavior or communication style.

Each of these harms on its own erodes belonging; combined, they create environments where students learn to shrink themselves to avoid constant correction or exclusion. This is why respect must be defined and operationalized through an intersectional lens (Ladson-Billings, 1995; Pinckney, 2021). It's not just about *acknowledging* identity—it's about removing the structural barriers that make identity a risk factor for harm.

Institutionalizing Respect

While classroom-level changes matter, students like Ray and Reagan also need systemic support. Respect must be embedded into school and district infrastructure, not left to the discretion of individual teachers. Key institutional practices include

- **Policy:** Gender identity and pronoun policies should explicitly require respect for names, pronouns, and gender expression, with clear accountability measures for violations (Human Rights Campaign, 2024b).
- **Reporting systems:** Put in place anonymous, accessible systems for reporting microaggressions, bullying, and identity-based harassment, with transparent follow-up processes.
- **Training:** Offer ongoing—not one-time—staff development on culturally relevant pedagogy, decolonizing classroom management, and racial justice-informed trans pedagogy (Mendoza & Johnson, 2024; Padayachee & Kriger, 2024).
- **Curriculum integration:** Embed LGBTQIA+ history, literature, and contributions throughout the year, not just during Pride Month or special events (Bigelow, 2022).

Institutionalizing respect ensures that a student's dignity is not contingent on whether they happen to have a Mr. Morales in their classroom.

Centering Student Agency

In both Ray's and Reagan's stories, the adult initiates the change. While this is often necessary, sustainable cultures of respect must also center youth leadership. As Queer Youth Assemble's (2023) *List of Demands* outlines, young people are calling for structural roles in shaping school culture.

Ways to embed student agency:

- **Student-led training:** Equip and pay students to lead professional learning for staff on pronouns, gender inclusion, and anti-bias practices.
- **Peer accountability systems:** Train peer leaders to mediate harm, offer bystander intervention, and build inclusive norms.
- **Youth equity councils:** Create formal groups of diverse students empowered to review school policies, advise on curriculum, and hold leadership accountable.

When students most impacted by disrespect have the power to shape norms, they shift the culture from the inside out—making respect a shared responsibility rather than a top-down expectation.

FIGURE 4.1
Who Holds the Power in Respect Building?

Role	Primary Powers and Responsibilities	Key BRAVE Alignment
Educators	Model inclusive language, interrupt harm in real time, create rituals of belonging, advocate for policy change.	Belonging, Respect, Advocacy
School Leaders	Set policies that protect LGBTQIA+ youth, allocate resources for training, hold staff accountable for bias/harm.	Respect, Advocacy, Visibility
Students	Co-create respect norms, lead peer accountability circles, provide feedback on school climate, model allyship.	Belonging, Visibility, Empathy
Families and Caregivers	Reinforce respect practices at home, partner with schools on affirming strategies, challenge harmful narratives.	Advocacy, Empathy
Community Partners	Offer affirming spaces beyond school, provide training/resources, amplify student voice in public forums.	Visibility, Advocacy, Belonging

Respect becomes systemic only when *all five groups* in Figure 4.1 see themselves as responsible for it. Concentrating power solely in adults reinforces top-down compliance models. Distributing power invites shared accountability—and makes respect a living, community practice rather than a rule to follow.

Respect in Action: A Tiered Framework for Every Educator

Respect isn't just about kindness—it's about building a school culture where LGBTQIA+ and neurodivergent youth are not merely "included" but deeply honored in their identities, communication styles, and ways of moving through the world. Too often, respect is framed as politeness or compliance. In truly inclusive environments, respect is proactive, intersectional, and embedded in both classroom practice and institutional systems.

The Tiered Respect Strategies Framework in Figure 4.2 offers a practical, scalable roadmap for educators at every level—from general education teachers to specialists, special educators, and service providers. It is designed to help you start where you are and expand your practice over time, moving from universal culture-building strategies to targeted supports, restorative responses, and systemic change.

FIGURE 4.2

Tiered Respect Strategies Framework for All Learners

Tier	Focus	Strategies for All Educators	Specialist/SPED Examples	Sample Script or Prompt
Tier 1: Universal Respect Practices *Creating a culture where every identity belongs*	Benefits all learners, especially LGBTQIA+ and neurodivergent students	• Use student-chosen names and pronouns consistently. • Greet students warmly at the door using non-gendered group labels ("Good morning, artists!"). • Normalize communication differences (AAC devices, scripting, stimming). • Offer multiple engagement modes (oral, written, visual, movement). • Build a norm-setting ritual collaboratively ("How do we want to be treated here?"). • Display inclusive signage and symbols (pronoun guides, neurodiversity pride, "This space affirms *all* bodies and brains").	**Music/Art:** Let students choose songs/art tied to their identity or cultural heritage. **PE:** Provide choices between group and individual activities; include sensory-safe warmups. **SPED:** Use storyboards and visuals that affirm both LGBTQIA+ and communication diversity.	"In this class, we celebrate different ways of thinking, creating, moving, and expressing who we are. There's no one right way to be human."
Tier 2: Targeted Respect Strategies *Centering the needs of LGBTQIA+ and neurodivergent youth*	Responds to the specific needs of students navigating marginalization	• Correct misgendering, deadnaming, or ableist language clearly ("Jas uses they/them pronouns—let's honor that."). • Build individualized support plans with student input. • Offer advisory/morning meeting prompts ("What's something people assume about you that isn't true?"). • Give choices in participation and group work. • Protect identity expression in all plans and goals.	**Art:** Assign a "My Truth" collage or identity exploration prompts. **Music:** Offer sensory-friendly instruments or nonverbal expression tools. **PE:** Use visual schedules, partner choice, and opt-ins for high-sensory activities. **SPED:** Avoid behavior goals that erase identity (masking gender presentation).	"We respect all ways of communicating here—speaking, typing, signing, drawing, moving. Every way counts."
Tier 3: Intensive and Restorative Practices *Repairing harm and redesigning the system*	Addresses harm caused by disrespect, microaggressions, or systemic failures	• Host restorative conversations centering the harmed student ("What would healing look like for you here?"). • Prioritize the needs of the harmed student over focus on the person causing harm. • Revise rules or supports that penalize differences. • Apply Universal Design for Learning (UDL) to reduce ableism. • Decolonize responses: resist urgency, perfectionism, and punitive isolation.	**Music/Art:** Use restorative circles after harm; showcase underrepresented voices. **PE:** Avoid public callouts; let students set teamwork norms. **SPED:** Pause IEPs to ensure identity-affirming language is present; invite student voice into IEPs.	"Have I assumed a student is 'noncompliant,' or are they communicating in a different way?"

FIGURE 4.2
Tiered Respect Strategies Framework for All Learners *(continued)*

Tier	Focus	Strategies for All Educators	Specialist/SPED Examples	Sample Script or Prompt
Tier 4: Systemic Respect Practices *Embedding respect into policies, professional learning, and adult culture for long-term sustainability*	Addresses the systemwide policies, professional learning, and adult culture needed to make respect sustainable and embedded across the entire school community	• Advocate for identity-affirming district policies (gender-inclusive dress codes, LGBTQIA+ curriculum integration, bias reporting protocols). • Lead professional learning for colleagues on culturally responsive and neurodiversity-affirming practices. • Partner with families, caregivers, and community organizations to co-create inclusive events and resources. • Build staff affinity groups and mentorship networks for marginalized educators. • Embed respect into hiring practices, staff handbooks, and discipline codes.	**Art/Music:** Host districtwide exhibits or performances featuring LGBTQIA+ and neurodivergent voices; integrate inclusive artists into curriculum maps. **PE:** Collaborate with district health teams to ensure adaptive PE programs affirm all bodies and abilities. **SPED**: Lead professional development on identity-affirming IEP language and family partnership models.	"As a school, we commit to respect, not as a one-time lesson, but as a culture sustained through our policies, curriculum, and adult actions. How will we hold ourselves accountable to this work over time?"

- Tier 1: Universal respect practices establish the baseline culture where every identity belongs. These are the everyday moves that tell students, "This is a place where you matter."
- Tier 2: Targeted respect strategies respond to the unique needs of marginalized students, whether related to gender identity, communication style, race, or neurotype.
- Tier 3: Intensive and restorative practices repair harm when it occurs and address the systems that allowed it.
- Tier 4: Systemic respect practices embed respect into policies, professional learning, and adult culture to ensure sustainability.

This framework is not meant to be linear—you may move between tiers daily. A PE teacher might implement a Tier 1 greeting in the morning, a Tier 2 adaptation in the afternoon, and a Tier 3 restorative conversation after lunch. The point is not perfection; it's commitment.

The table in Figure 4.3 distills the most impactful practices from each tier, with examples that are easy to adapt across content areas and service

FIGURE 4.3

Leadership and Systemic Respect Practices for School and District Leaders

Action Area	Guiding Questions	Next Steps
Audit Language and Policies	• Do our handbooks affirm diverse identities? • Are misgendering and deadnaming explicitly identified as harmful? • Are neurodivergent communication styles acknowledged and protected?	Form a student advisory group (including LGBTQIA+ and neurodivergent youth) to review and revise documents.
Elevate Identity-Informed PD	• Are we moving beyond compliance into lived-experience learning? • Are facilitators representative of communities served?	Budget annually for queer/trans and disability justice-led workshops; integrate them into leadership PD plans.
Create Brave Space Agreements for Staff	• Do adults model respect daily? • Are microaggressions addressed as learning moments?	Facilitate staff co-creation of agreements; post in shared spaces; reflect monthly in team meetings.

models. Use it as a checklist, a planning tool, and a reflection guide. Whether you're a classroom teacher, a music specialist, a school leader, or a paraeducator, you'll find actions you can take tomorrow that make respect visible and nonnegotiable.

Respect Is a Two-Way Street

Systemic respect starts with naming the defaults we've inherited—and choosing differently. The unwritten rules of schooling often reflect values rooted in white supremacy culture: control over curiosity, compliance over connection, comfort over courage. But respect cannot be reduced to obedience. It is a relational act, a living practice, and a form of justice.

The tiered strategies in this chapter are not "extras." They are the daily moves that shift respect from theory to practice—especially for students navigating overlapping forms of marginalization. For queer, trans, BIPOC, and neurodivergent youth, each layer of identity can increase exposure to bias, microaggressions, and disproportionate discipline (Ladson-Billings, 1995; Pinckney, 2021). The stakes are not abstract; they are lived in every hallway glance, mispronounced name, or disciplinary referral that could have been a conversation.

When students like Reagan are met with harm—through misgendering, dismissal, or invisibility—they are not just experiencing a personal slight. They are bumping up against systems that have not yet reckoned with the following questions: *Whose humanity is protected here? Whose identity is centered?*

Educators cannot always change the system overnight. But we can change how we show up within it. Respect begins when we choose to unlearn the norms that harm, reimagine our rituals of power, and build classrooms rooted in the BRAVE framework:

- **Belonging:** Creating spaces where students are not asked to conform to be accepted.
- **Respect:** Honoring identity as nonnegotiable and not conditional.
- **Advocacy:** Speaking up when harm happens—even when it's uncomfortable.
- **Visibility:** Making our allyship legible through language, environment, and practice.
- **Empathy:** Listening not to fix but to witness and believe.

Importantly, respect building cannot be adult-only work. Brave cultures grow stronger when students co-create the norms, lead restorative conversations, and design accountability structures that reflect their lived realities. From youth equity councils to student-led professional learning for staff, young people must be positioned as architects—not just beneficiaries—of respect.

Mr. Morales didn't wait for a schoolwide policy to act. He moved with clarity, care, and courage—choosing to shift the soil so brave seeds like Reagan could take root. That is what brave respect looks like in practice: not a perfect script but a posture of accountability, listening, and repair.

Respect is a two-way street—but in schools, it must begin with us. Students like Reagan should never have to prove their humanity before they receive ours.

Key Takeaways

- Respect is not neutrality—it's action. It demands disrupting bias and inequity, not just tolerating difference.
- Many "respect" norms are rooted in assimilation. In too many schools, expectations mirror white, cisgender, neurotypical, and heteronormative values. BRAVE educators examine and dismantle these defaults.
- Respect for neurodivergent, queer, and trans students must be intentional. It requires practices that are responsive, inclusive, and rooted in genuine relationships.
- Ancestral community practices are blueprints for liberation. Talking circles, call-and-response, storytelling, and shared wisdom rituals model ways to build belonging and respect that predate colonial norms.
- BRAVE educators act without waiting for permission. They begin with their own sphere of influence—one classroom, one team, one student relationship at a time.

BRAVE Reflection Questions

Use these for personal reflection, team learning, or schoolwide inquiry:

- **Belonging:** What messages—verbal, nonverbal, structural—tell students who truly belong in our space?
- **Respect:** Are our norms built on mutual care, or on control and compliance?
- **Advocacy:** When have I interrupted harm? When have I stayed silent? Why?
- **Visibility:** What daily signals—visual, verbal, relational—tell queer, trans, and neurodivergent students they are safe here?
- **Empathy:** How often do I pause to hear what students need—without defending myself, the policy, or the system?

Chapter 4 Playlist

Visit www.ccmeducationgroup.co to access a curated collection of resources designed to support you in building a culture of brave respect in your classroom and school community:

- Tools to audit policies for white-normative and gendered language.
- Restorative and decolonized classroom management strategies.
- Inclusive language guides for queer, trans, and neurodivergent students.
- Brave storytelling from educators and youth navigating identity, harm, and healing.
- Specialist resources for art, music, PE, and SPED educators.
- PD toolkits on transgender studies, disability justice, and BIPOC-led practices.

Advocacy Is a Verb

"Advocacy is not just about speaking up—it's about listening deeply, challenging systems, and risking comfort for someone else's liberation."
—Raquel Willis

The Legacy That Lit the Flame

Before Stonewall, before rainbow flags lined city streets, there was Compton's Cafeteria—a small diner in San Francisco's Tenderloin District where, in 1966, trans women of color, drag queens, and queer youth gathered for warmth, safety, and community. It was a space where they could exhale—until the police raids came. One summer night, after yet another round of harassment, one woman hurled her cup of coffee into an officer's face. In an instant, the room erupted. Glass shattered. Tables overturned. Voices rose into the night. It was not just a riot—it was a refusal to disappear.

Among those shaped by that defiance was Miss Major Griffin-Gracy, a Black trans elder whose activism carried the flame from Compton's Cafeteria to the Stonewall Uprising and well beyond. In a 2023 interview with *The*

Guardian, she reflected on the spaces she's fought to build: "When the girls come here, they don't have to worry about anything. . . . I've gotta make joy here, because it doesn't exist in the normal world" (Levin, 2023). In Miss Major's words, joy is not frivolous—it is survival. It is a protest. It is a deliberate act of care in a world designed to deny it.

Three years after Compton's, in the summer of 1969, the fight reignited at the Stonewall Inn. When police once again raided a queer gathering space, LGBTQIA+ patrons—many of them Black and Latine trans women, street kids, and gender-nonconforming youth—stood their ground. What followed was not a singular "moment" but six nights of uprising, grief, joy, rage, and resilience. For decades, the story was distilled into the search for a "first brick." But as artists and historians like Tourmaline remind us, myths flatten the truth: "We don't need myths to make our history matter. We need to remember that advocacy was—and still is—collective" (Reign, 2018).

Advocacy did not begin at Stonewall, and it certainly did not end there. It has always been an accumulation of pain, protest, and possibility—a steady beat of resistance carried by those who refused to be erased by systems built for their invisibility. Filmmaker and activist Tourmaline's own organizing work was shaped by the everyday realities of trans survival in New York City. "Often when trans people go to the welfare office, the person working would say, 'No, come back when you look like a man,' or 'No, come back when you look like a woman,'" she explained, noting that access to benefits is a matter of life and death when "being barred from work and job discrimination" leave few options (Reign, 2018).

Her research into Marsha P. Johnson's life uncovered a "really large legacy of fighting back at Stonewall" and leading HIV/AIDS activism in the early 1990s. Yet she also saw "a particular kind of anti-Black historical erasure" obscuring Marsha's role and contributions (Reign, 2018). This is why telling our stories matters—not to cling to singular myths but to connect with our lineage, to draw strength from it, and to use it as fuel for present-day care work. As Tourmaline reminds us, "The things that other people deem not of consequence or not mattering actually really matter a lot . . . small acts of fighting back, of resisting the status quo, and being unruly have huge impacts" (Reign, 2018).

Her co-director, Sasha Wortzel, put it plainly: advocacy is sustained by "feeling connected to a lineage, connected to ancestors . . . knowing that we've always been powerful in making community and place and changing the world through large and small acts" (Reign, 2018). This work is as much about marching in the streets as it is about the quiet gestures—cooking a meal for someone, making a phone call to check in, saying, *I see you. What do you need?*

In the end, advocacy is not an identity—it's a practice. A verb. A way of moving through the world that insists no one is disposable, and everyone has a role in the work of liberation.

What Advocacy Really Means

Advocacy is the courageous and consistent act of standing in solidarity with those pushed to the margins—especially when it costs us something. It is not symbolic. It's not a celebration once a year. And it certainly isn't something we outsource to one teacher, one GSA advisor, or one DEI committee. Advocacy is a daily muscle—built through conscious acts of interruption, amplification, repair, and redesign. In education, advocacy means interrupting harm, redistributing power, and redesigning systems to center those historically erased or silenced.

It means we step in when a student is misgendered. It means we audit policies that punish Black queer students for their hairstyles or their hoodies. It means we stop using "ally" as a title and start using it as a verb.

The stakes are high. According to GLSEN's (2024) National School Climate Survey:

- Nearly 75 percent of LGBTQIA+ students hear homophobic remarks at school.
- More than half feel unsafe due to their sexual orientation or gender expression.
- Only one in five students attend a school with an inclusive curriculum or explicitly supportive policies.
- Trans and nonbinary youth of color face disproportionately high rates of suspension, misidentification, and educational pushout.

This data is not new—and for many educators and students, it's not abstract. It's lived.

"Last year, I had to lead a workshop just to get my school to start using my name," said Jordan, a nonbinary 10th grader in Massachusetts. "It felt like I had to prove I existed before I could even ask for respect" (GLSEN, 2024).

Jordan's story is not an outlier. It is the present-day echo of decades of forced resilience—a resilience students never asked for. And just as advocacy demands we affirm queer and trans lives, it also calls us to dismantle ableist norms and decolonize the very metrics we use to define belonging. Neurodiverse students are too often asked to "mask" in the name of classroom compliance. BIPOC queer youth are told their identities are "too political" for school assemblies. And students with disabilities are frequently left out of conversations about equity and inclusion—despite being central to them.

What's more, advocacy doesn't begin and end with gender and sexuality. It must also disrupt ableist norms and decolonize the metrics we use to define worthiness and belonging. Neurodivergent students are often punished for not masking their identities. Disabled students are silenced by environments that treat accessibility as an afterthought. And too often, students who exist at the intersection of queerness, Blackness, and disability are told that their very presence is "too political" for assemblies, student leadership, or curricular inclusion.

As Lydia X. Z. Brown, a disability justice scholar, reminds us, "Ableism is everywhere. Disability justice calls on us to fight this, to develop a deliberate consciousness—it is inherently intersectional" (Callahan, 2018, para. 26). And as Dr. Gholdy Muhammad (2020) teaches in her framework for historically responsive education, belonging is not just about making space. It's about cultivating genius, joy, and identity in young people—especially those who have been historically erased by dominant norms.

So what does advocacy require in our schools? It requires us to step in—when a student is misgendered in class, when a policy criminalizes hoodies and hairstyles, when a neurodivergent learner is reprimanded for not making eye contact. It asks us to do more than declare ourselves allies. We must be active as allies.

It requires us to move from intention to action, from belief to behavior, from silence to solidarity. This chapter is your invitation to do just that. To move from remembering resistance to enacting it. To transform your role—whether as a classroom teacher, school leader, or district decision maker—

into a platform for redistributing power and rebuilding belonging. You don't need to be perfect. You just need to be accountable. And willing. Respect without advocacy is performance. But advocacy, practiced consistently and collectively? That's liberation.

From the Steps of Stonewall to the Steps of the State House

If Compton's Cafeteria lit the flame and Stonewall kept it burning, today's queer and trans youth are carrying that fire forward—refusing to be erased by systems that still fail to see them.

In March 2023, ahead of Trans Day of Visibility, queer and trans youth from across Massachusetts gathered outside the State House. They didn't come just to be seen. They came to demand change. Organized by the Massachusetts Commission on LGBTQ Youth (MCLGBTQY), the rally centered student voices—young people who had spent their school years being misnamed, mislabeled, and made invisible.

One student stepped to the mic and said, "This isn't symbolic. This is our life. We need policies, practices, and school spaces that don't keep us hidden" (Bennett, 2023).

These students didn't just rally—they presented formal legislative recommendations to state leaders, calling for LGBTQIA-inclusive curricula, safer schools, affirming healthcare access, and protections for trans and nonbinary youth of color in K–12 settings (Massachusetts Commission on LGBTQ Youth, 2025). Their actions weren't random. They were radical. They were rooted in the legacy of those who fought before them. And this wasn't just happening in Boston.

That same year, outside the U.S. Supreme Court, queer youth staged a vocal and visible protest in response to a ruling allowing parents to opt students out of LGBTQIA-inclusive literature and curriculum. Holding signs that read, "We Belong in Every Book," students made their message clear: queer visibility is not optional. It is essential.

"This ruling tells us our identities are debatable," one protester told the press. "We dissent—not because we're angry, but because we're alive" (Queer Youth Assemble, 2023).

Across the country, school districts are beginning to listen. Some have implemented student-designed training for faculty on gender inclusion. Others have partnered with advocacy groups like BAGLY to develop year-round programming—not just Pride Week posters but leadership summits, health workshops, and mental wellness circles created *by* youth *for* youth.

These aren't fringe stories. They are frontline blueprints. They remind us that advocacy in education doesn't always look like a policy memo. Sometimes, it looks like a student demanding their pronouns be respected. Sometimes, it's a hallway conversation where an educator steps up. Other times, it's youth taking the mic on the front steps of Beacon Hill and telling the world they are not going anywhere. Just like the queens and street kids of Stonewall, they are declaring: *We exist. We resist. We lead.*

Common Pitfalls: Where Advocacy Falters

Advocacy is not passive. It's not performance. It is the sacred act of standing in the gap when the gap could cost you everything. Too often, what's labeled as advocacy in schools is not advocacy at all. It's intention without impact—symbolic gestures without systemic shifts. When we fail to confront the ways race, gender, and other identities intersect within systems of power, we reproduce the very inequities we claim to resist. In schools, that failure can look like an educator who displays a rainbow sticker but stays silent when a student is bullied for being gender-nonconforming. Or it can look like a district that drafts an equity statement while quietly disciplining students who challenge white, heteronormative norms. To move beyond symbolic advocacy, we must understand the common pitfalls—how they manifest and what they cost our students.

Silence

In classrooms and staff rooms, it can sound like nothing at all—just a tight-lipped pause after a student is misgendered or a sidelong glance when a colleague makes a racially coded joke. But that silence says everything. It sends clear, if unspoken, messages: *Your identity is negotiable. Your pain is too much. Your presence is a problem to be managed, not honored.*

The impulse to stay silent isn't always rooted in malice. More often, it emerges from fear, uncertainty, or exhaustion. As Esther Ohito (2024) observes, educators operate in systems saturated with racialized and gendered power dynamics, where speaking out can provoke professional or personal risk—especially for those already marginalized. For some, silence becomes a survival strategy, not a sign of indifference.

Still, the costs of that survival strategy are high. Students see and feel our silences. They learn quickly who will speak up for them and who will not. Over time, silence can erode trust just as powerfully as overt acts of harm.

Ohito's (2024) research identifies several forces that shape whether an educator intervenes or stays quiet:

- **Institutional culture:** Schools with unclear policies or a history of punishing those who speak out create a climate of fear.
- **Collegial dynamics:** Educators may hesitate to challenge peers, especially if it risks professional relationships or job security.
- **Personal identity and positionality:** Those from historically marginalized backgrounds often carry additional calculations—navigating the dual risks of speaking as "the only" and the backlash for challenging dominant norms.
- **Psychological safety:** Without trust in leadership and colleagues, the emotional labor of speaking up can feel like a solitary, and dangerous, act.

In practice, this means that even values-aligned educators can find themselves in what Ohito calls *conflicted complicity*—moments where one's ethics urge action, but the perceived threat of retaliation, isolation, or futility tips the scale toward inaction. For educators, this is not just an individual challenge but a structural one. Our silence is often the by-product of policies, practices, and cultures that fail to protect or empower those who speak out. That's why shifting from silence to advocacy is not simply about personal courage—it's about redesigning the conditions so that speaking up is not an act of martyrdom but a shared, expected practice of care.

Or, as one veteran teacher in Ohito's study put it: "When I know my school has my back, I can have my students' backs. When I know it doesn't, I think twice—and the students can feel that."

BRAVE Reflection: Breaking the Silence in Our Schools

Silence is not neutral. In classrooms and staff rooms, it can sound like nothing—but it says everything. It tells students: *Your identity is negotiable. Your pain is too much. Your presence is a problem to be managed, not honored.*

As Ohito (2024) reminds us, moments of educator inaction are rarely simple. Fear, moral injury, and the absence of psychological safety can all lead to what she calls *self-protective silence*—a survival response that can look like passivity but is actually a calculated choice to endure rather than risk harm.

Yet silence, no matter how well-intentioned, leaves students to carry the weight of injustice alone.

Reflect:

- When have I stayed silent in the face of harm—and why?
- What internal or external risks shaped my decision to remain quiet?
- Who is most affected when I choose self-protection over intervention?
- What small, immediate actions could replace my silence with solidarity?

Action Step: Identify one recurring harm in your school (e.g., misgendering, racially coded jokes, inaccessible learning materials) and commit to *interrupting it every time.* Tell a colleague your plan so they can hold you accountable.

Compassion Fatigue

Educators are tired—but not just from grading, planning, or navigating pandemic-era logistics. Many are experiencing what the research identifies as *compassion fatigue*: a state of emotional, cognitive, and spiritual exhaustion caused by sustained exposure to others' pain, especially in caregiving roles.

As Ensz (2021) explains, compassion fatigue develops when teachers and leaders internalize the suffering of students without sufficient time, tools, or support to process what they're holding. This is especially prevalent in schools serving communities affected by systemic inequities, where trauma is not the exception but the backdrop.

During the COVID-19 pandemic, school leaders across the country reported profound emotional depletion. Alyami and Ghamri (2023) found that principals who were deeply committed to justice-oriented work experienced heightened levels of helplessness, professional isolation, and burnout—often without clear institutional mechanisms for recovery.

This isn't the same as burnout from workload. It's the grief that accumulates when educators care deeply but feel unsupported in translating that care into sustainable action. Compassion fatigue whispers: *I still care . . . but I can't keep going like this.*

For students, the consequences are not invisible. In Chapter 4, we met Reagan, a biracial, gender-nonconforming 4th grader who had begun to shrink in the face of cisnormative expectations. "I just want to be good," Reagan told Mr. Morales quietly one afternoon, "so people stop looking at me weird." Reagan's desire to disappear wasn't about compliance—it was about relief. In schools where adults are too depleted to advocate, students often choose invisibility as protection.

Shame, Paralysis, and Assimilation

Underneath silence and fatigue often lies a deeper wound: *shame*. Brené Brown (2021) defines shame as the belief that we are unworthy of love, connection, or belonging. In schools, shame surfaces when we realize we've caused harm, when a peer calls us in or out, or when we freeze in moments that demand bravery. The sting of being exposed—especially in front of colleagues or students—can push educators toward self-protection rather than re-engagement. Instead of leaning back into the work, we shrink, avoiding the very conversations where our presence matters most.

When shame fuses with fear, paralysis often follows. This freeze response isn't born of indifference but of internal conflict. The mind races with ruminations: *What if I say the wrong thing again? What if I'm labeled harmful? What if I lose my credibility or my job?* Psychologists call this *narrative looping*—replaying a mistake or hypothetical over and over until avoidance feels safer than action. Without tools, practice, and collective accountability, this state can linger, turning moments of potential advocacy into missed opportunities for justice.

This paralysis has a downstream effect on students, often leading to assimilation. When students see adults retreat from advocacy, they learn a dangerous lesson: *Survival means self-erasure.* Esther Ohito (2024) describes this as a pattern in white-dominant educational spaces where "every silenced moment becomes an unspoken lesson about which version of themselves is welcome—and which is not" (p. 12). Over time, students begin reshaping their language, dress, interests, and identities to avoid being targeted or excluded.

Harm runs deep; identities do not exist in isolation. For students navigating the compounded vulnerabilities of race, gender, sexuality, class, and ability, every act of assimilation extracts a cost. Crenshaw (1991) reminds us that those forced to adapt "feel the cost of accommodation more fully" because their survival often requires navigating multiple systems of oppression at once.

Shame, paralysis, and assimilation are not inevitable outcomes—they are data points. They tell us where fear lives in our systems and where we must build the skills, relationships, and courage to re-engage. Silence may feel safe in the moment, but for our students, it's a lesson in invisibility they should never have to learn.

Case Study: Ms. O'Malley—From Silence to Stepping In

Ms. O'Malley, a white, cisgender former middle school English teacher in Baton Rouge, Louisiana, has recently stepped into her first year as principal at a diverse yet politically complex middle school. The district promotes "community values" and "academic excellence," but unwritten rules about what can and cannot be named in public spaces linger in the air.

Years before, while still teaching, Ms. O'Malley sat in a small-group discussion when a student misgendered Alex, a nonbinary classmate who uses she/they pronouns. The comment was sharp, the pause afterward sharper. She felt her pulse quicken, her chest tighten—she *knew* it was wrong.

But then came the rush of questions: *What if I say the wrong thing? What if I make it worse? What if this spirals into a call from an angry parent?* The moment slipped by. Class moved on. And in the quiet of her car that afternoon, she replayed it, realizing she had taught a lesson without meaning to—that it was safer to say nothing.

In hindsight, Ms. O'Malley understood she wasn't indifferent. She was stuck in the space this chapter names: shame and paralysis. She felt shame that she had let the moment go and paralysis from the fear of compounding harm or losing credibility.

Over time, she saw how her silence didn't just protect herself—it demanded assimilation from her students. For Alex, it meant adjusting their identity to fit into a classroom that didn't yet know how to hold it.

Now, as a principal, she carries that moment with her. She's begun to see how assimilation happens not just for students but for adults too—when leaders bite their tongue in staff meetings, water down equity goals, or defer advocacy until "a better time."

She's committed to doing it differently, but she knows commitment is not the same as action. She is learning that advocacy is not just a value; it's a practiced skill. And it requires leaning into discomfort, even when her body says, *Stay quiet.*

Reflection for leaders:

- When have you felt shame or fear silence you?
- How might your hesitation contribute—intentionally or not—to student or staff assimilation?
- How do respect and belonging (from Chapters 2 and 3) show up in the way you respond to harm in real time?
- What would it take for your advocacy to be instinct, not an afterthought?

What Helped Ms. O'Malley

After that moment of pause—when she hesitated to use Alex's pronouns—Ms. O'Malley could have done what so many do in moments of harm: retreat into shame, rationalize the misstep, or bury the discomfort under "good intentions."

She didn't.

What brought her back wasn't a compliance module or a reprimanding email. It was restorative dialogue and professional learning grounded in identity work—delivered in a space that allowed her to be human *and* accountable.

Later that week, during a staff learning circle, Mr. Morales facilitated a conversation on missteps and mending. The invitation wasn't to perform allyship—it was to *practice* it. "We're going to get it wrong sometimes," he reminded them. "But the goal isn't perfection. It's repair."

The discussion moved from defensiveness to reflection, from "I didn't mean to" toward "What can I do differently next time?" Colleagues named their fears and discomforts out loud—without shame being weaponized against them.

For Ms. O'Malley, this was a turning point: "It wasn't just that I was forgiven. Someone believed I could do better—and gave me the space to try."

In the weeks that followed, she not only affirmed Alex publicly in class but also pushed for gender-inclusive professional development at a department meeting. She moved from pause to practice, from shame to solidarity.

Her journey mirrors the arc many educators crave: the will to act, met with the tools, time, and trust to try again.

Advocacy in Everyday Moments

When we think about advocacy, we often picture rallies, protests, or public statements. But in schools, advocacy often arrives quietly—hidden inside passing comments, curriculum choices, hallway interactions, and meeting protocols. These moments rarely give you time to prepare, and they almost never come with clear instructions.

Advocacy in these spaces isn't about a single grand gesture—it's about a pattern of choices. Choices to speak or to stay silent. To affirm or to avoid. To risk discomfort in service of dignity.

As Kimberlé Crenshaw (1991) reminds us, the stakes are highest for those whose identities live at the intersections of multiple oppressions. In schools, this means that hesitation or silence from adults doesn't just maintain the status quo—it teaches students which parts of themselves are welcome and which parts they must hide.

The following vignettes illustrate the small but significant advocacy moments that educators encounter every day. None of these take place in the spotlight. They happen in the spaces where culture is made—in staff lounges, in inboxes, in team meetings. And in each moment, the educator must choose: freeze, fumble, or speak.

Vignette 1: The Staff Lounge Shrug

At a suburban middle school, Ms. Patel overheard a colleague joke during lunch: "Pretty soon every kid will come out as gay just for attention."

Laughter. Shrugs. Ms. Patel froze. She didn't laugh—but she didn't speak either.

Later, she told her mentor, "I just didn't want to make it awkward."

Her mentor replied, "It was already awkward. You just didn't make it better."

The next morning, Ms. Patel slipped a handwritten note into her colleague's mailbox: "Sexuality isn't a punchline. If we expect students to trust us with who they are, we have to show respect even when they're not around."

The jokes stopped. At the next staff meeting, she proposed a student-led panel on LGBTQIA+ experiences in schools.

Vignette 2: The Parent Email

After assigning a poem by a queer Black author, Mr. Rivera received a parent email: "I don't want my child learning about that lifestyle in school."

He sat with it for hours. His hands trembled as he typed—but he grounded himself in this truth: representation is not indoctrination; it's belonging.

His reply: "Our responsibility is to reflect the diversity of the world our students live in. That includes LGBTQIA+ voices, stories, and lives. If your child has questions, I'm here to support them. But we will not erase anyone's humanity."

Days later, a student slipped him a sticky note: "Thank you for sharing that poem. It made me feel like my story mattered."

Vignette 3: The Assistant Principal's Dilemma

In a health class planning meeting, a teacher casually referred to Riley as "going through a phase" after Riley had shared openly in class about having a boyfriend. Riley, the only openly queer student in the grade, was sitting right there.

Ms. Nguyen, the assistant principal, froze for a moment. Speaking up might spark staff defensiveness; saying nothing would signal agreement. She exhaled.

"For the purposes of this meeting—and Riley's dignity—we honor what students share about themselves. Sexuality isn't a phase. It's who they are. Our job is to create a classroom where they feel safe."

Later, Riley emailed her: "You didn't even flinch. I'll never forget that."

From Small Moments to Lasting Change

These stories aren't about grand gestures or breaking news—they're about hallway decisions, quiet corrections, and choosing to speak when silence feels safer. Advocacy doesn't always happen at the microphone or in front of a protest banner. More often, it's in the staff lounge, the email reply, or the meeting where everyone else is looking down at their notes.

What connects Ms. Patel, Mr. Rivera, and Ms. Nguyen is not that they acted perfectly—it's that they acted at all. Their responses disrupted patterns that often go unchecked. They made choices that, in small but meaningful ways, affirmed someone's humanity in real time. And just like Ms. O'Malley in Baton Rouge, each of them had to confront the same pressures that keep many educators quiet: fear of conflict, fear of getting it wrong, and fear of being isolated.

Why Advocacy Feels Risky

We can't talk about speaking up without naming what holds us back. Educators operate within systems where

- Fear of backlash—from colleagues, families, or leadership—can be career-defining.
- Exhaustion makes constant vigilance feel unsustainable.
- Assimilation can masquerade as "professionalism," convincing us to mute parts of ourselves.
- Uncertainty about when or how to intervene can lead to silence in the moment.

Recognizing these barriers doesn't excuse inaction—it helps us understand why advocacy often requires courage *and* community.

A Framework for Micro-Advocacy

When your heart is pounding, it helps to have a structure to lean on. Think of it as muscle memory for moments when you can't script the scene in advance:

1. **Pause:** Take a breath to ground yourself before responding.
2. **Name:** State what you heard or saw: "I want to pause us there—what was just said could be harmful."

3. **Bridge:** Connect it to a shared value: "Our students' dignity and trust depend on what we say about them when they're not in the room."
4. **Commit:** Identify the next step: "Let's revisit this in our next meeting so we can address it as a team."

These steps don't guarantee comfort—but they create clarity. And clarity, over time, builds culture.

Everyday Scripts for Educators

These aren't just lines to memorize. They're invitations to interrupt harm and signal that identity matters—even when you're still learning.

- **When you make a mistake:** "I want to pause and apologize—I used the wrong name/pronouns. I see you, and I'll keep working to get it right."
- **When a student is harmed:** "That comment was not OK. In this space, we honor each other's identities. Let's pause and talk about what respect looks like here."
- **When colleagues struggle:** "This might be uncomfortable, but it matters. Can we revisit that conversation? I noticed something we may need to unpack."
- **To signal advocacy proactively:** "Your name. Your pronouns. Your story. They matter here. If I mess up, please know I'm open to feedback—and I'm committed to learning."

Leadership Practices That Model BRAVE Advocacy

If we want advocacy to thrive, we must build conditions that sustain it—especially in systems where resistance is met with risk.

1. **Normalize imperfection and repair:** Create professional learning spaces where vulnerability is modeled and repair is practiced. Use case studies (like Ms. O'Malley's) in professional development—not to shame but to show what growth looks like in motion.
2. **Invest in peer coaching circles:** Educators often learn best from one another. Facilitate affinity-based and cross-role coaching circles where teachers can process complex moments, rehearse scripts, and lean into one another's wisdom.

3. **Build responsive accountability structures:** Instead of punishing harm, restore community. Use harm acknowledgment forms, student-led forums, and restorative response teams that center the experiences of those most affected.
4. **Embed advocacy in evaluation:** Shift educator evaluation rubrics to include indicators related to equity leadership, identity-affirming practice, and inclusive classroom culture. Make advocacy part of the job—not an extra for the willing few.
5. **Develop crisis protocols that center student dignity:** Whether a student is outed without consent, a slur is written on a locker, or a parent files a complaint about an inclusive book, school leaders need clear, trauma-informed protocols that prioritize safety over optics and healing over image control.

What Youth Say They Actually Need

Across the country, queer and trans youth are not only resisting—they're organizing, educating, creating art, leading policy conversations, and building community on their own terms. Their message is unapologetically clear: symbolic gestures are not enough.

Pride posters in June, "safe space" stickers on a door, or the occasional rainbow-themed spirit day do not make a school inclusive. Visibility without protection is hollow. What these young people are calling for—often at great personal cost—is a fundamental shift in how schools see, hear, and support them. They want schools that are responsive, not performative; brave, not just safe.

LGBTQIA+ youth organizers in Boston, under the Queer Youth Assemble (2023) banner, released a comprehensive List of Demands for their schools and communities. These demands didn't emerge from a single protest—they were crafted through listening circles, peer-led advocacy trainings, and intergenerational town halls rooted in deep community wisdom. The demands were practical and visionary:

- Affirming, trauma-informed mental health support.
- LGBTQIA+-inclusive, medically accurate sex education.
- Queer and trans representation in curriculum across subjects.
- Gender-expansive bathroom and locker room policies.

- Pronoun and name recognition in student records and portals.
- Restorative practices over punitive discipline policies.
- Support for queer student clubs and paid stipends for faculty sponsors.

One student, speaking at the Boston Youth Pride Town Hall, said it plainly: "If we're expected to learn here, we should be allowed to exist here" (Queer Youth Assemble, 2023).

They weren't asking for perfection. They were asking to be protected.

Another student activist from Worcester added, "Adults keep asking us what we want. And we keep telling them. But listening isn't just hearing us—it's doing something with what we said."

This is the gap youth are calling out—not a gap in values, but a gap in action. Too often, schools respond to harm with statements instead of systems. Students can feel the difference.

As David J. Johns—former kindergarten teacher, CEO of the National Black Justice Coalition, and creator of *Teach Them Babies, the Podcast*—reminds us, "We don't need permission to exist. We need institutions to stop making us prove we're worthy of protection" (Burga, 2025a).

This insistence is rooted in ancestral resistance, but it's also intimately modern. Today's queer youth are growing up in a political climate increasingly hostile to their existence: anti-trans legislation, book bans, school censorship, and so-called Don't Say Gay laws attempt to erase their identities before they can even fully name them. But still—they show up.

Still—they organize sit-ins, walkouts, Instagram campaigns, mutual aid drives, and Pride celebrations that reclaim joy as resistance. They are creating community where systems have failed them. In one moving account, students at a California high school created a classroom zine series focused on queer joy and resistance as a way to heal from trauma and visibility fatigue. (Bigelow, 2022)

One student contributor wrote, "It's not that I want to be brave. It's that I've never been given another choice."

These are not abstract demands. They are living, actionable blueprints for the kind of advocacy young people need now: specific, sustained, and community-led. They're telling us how to be better educators, administrators, and allies—if we have the humility to listen and the courage to respond.

The youth are not asking adults to save them. They're asking adults to stand beside them, to risk something with them, to say: *You do not have to be brave alone.*

From Performative to Protective: Practicing Everyday Advocacy

Advocacy is not an abstract value—it's a lived, daily practice. It requires us to move beyond symbolic gestures toward systemic change that protects, affirms, and sustains queer and trans youth. As the stories in this chapter make clear, our job is not to "save" young people but to stand alongside them with humility, courage, and staying power.

When students call for gender-expansive bathrooms, inclusive curricula, or trauma-informed mental health supports, they are not asking for special treatment. They are asking for the basic conditions to exist, learn, and thrive. The stakes are not theoretical; they are embedded in every policy decision, staff interaction, and school tradition.

Ms. O'Malley's choice to return after harm was not perfection—it was protection. The youth-led demands from Boston to Baton Rouge remind us that advocacy must be responsive, not performative; protective, not conditional. And as David J. Johns reminds us, queer and trans youth of color deserve a future "where they don't have to be brave to simply exist" (Burga, 2025a).

Advocacy lives in the BRAVE framework:

- **Belonging:** Designing systems and spaces where students' full identities are affirmed, not erased.
- **Respect:** Responding to discomfort with curiosity and repair instead of silence or retreat.
- **Advocacy:** Making harm visible and acting to change the conditions that caused it.
- **Visibility:** Embedding queer and trans presence in curriculum, culture, and leadership.
- **Empathy:** Extending grace to others as freely as we wish to receive it ourselves.

Importantly, advocacy is not adult-only work. When students co-create safety plans, lead equity initiatives, or train staff on inclusive practices, they are modeling what systems-level courage looks like. Our task is to resource them, protect them, and stand in solidarity—not just in the easy moments but when it costs us something.

Brave advocacy begins with us. Young people should never have to risk their safety to prove they deserve protection.

Key Takeaways

- Advocacy is not passive agreement—it's active disruption of inequity.
- Symbolic gestures without structural change are hollow.
- Queer and trans youth of color have already defined what safety and joy look like; our role is to implement it.
- Everyday advocacy happens in lesson plans, hallway conversations, policies, and responses to harm.
- Brave advocacy starts with our own sphere of influence and grows outward.

BRAVE Reflection Questions

Use these for personal reflection, team dialogue, or professional learning:

- **Belonging:** What systems or routines in your school unintentionally exclude queer, trans, or gender-expansive youth—and how can you redesign them to affirm full identity expression?
- **Respect:** When discomfort arises—yours or others'—how do you hold space for learning without retreating into silence or shame?
- **Advocacy:** What is one practice, policy, or interaction you will commit to changing this month to make advocacy more than a value—but a verb?
- **Visibility:** Where are LGBTQIA+ students and educators reflected in your curriculum, visuals, and leadership—and where are they still erased?
- **Empathy:** When have you felt paralyzed by fear or shame—and what helped you come back? How might you extend that same grace to a colleague or student?

Chapter 5 Playlist

Visit www.ccmeducationgroup.co to access tools and narratives that support sustained, equity-driven advocacy:

- *List of Demands* from Queer Youth Assemble (2023).
- Student-led zine curriculum from *Rethinking Schools*.
- David Johns's article on queer Black joy as resistance.
- Advocacy repair scripts for educators and school leaders.
- Templates for inclusive name/pronoun policies.
- Professional learning activities for DEIB recommitment.

6

Visibility as Resistance, Ritual, and Refuge

"The category is: Live. Work. Pose."
—*Pray Tell, Pose*

Seeing Alex: The Courage to Be Seen

Alex wasn't always Alex.

She had been *Alexander* on every birth certificate, report card, and attendance sheet until middle school, when she shortened it—not to "blend in" but to buy herself breathing room. It was the safest way she knew to live with the gnawing truth she carried: that maybe she had been born in the wrong body.

Now a Black transgender girl in high school who uses she/they pronouns, Alex carried herself with a quiet defiance—headscarf wrapped high, rainbow pin fixed to her backpack—small signals to herself that she was still here. But each morning, the teacher's roll call pulled her back into a name she had shed, slicing the air with a reminder: *We still don't see you.*

The paperwork she had submitted—preferred name, correct pronouns—sat somewhere in a file, unprocessed or ignored. Her art was absent from hallway displays. Classmates' whispers trailed her in the cafeteria. And even when Principal O'Malley stopped by with a kind smile, Alex kept her guard up. She had learned the hard way that, in a school that claims to "welcome all," being visible could still mean being unsafe.

Principal O'Malley noticed her, though—more than Alex probably realized. She remembered what it felt like to shrink parts of herself just to survive, to camouflage her identity in a space where her very being felt like a provocation. Fresh from her years as a middle school English teacher, Ms. O'Malley was still learning what it meant to lead in a progressive-yet-conservative place like Baton Rouge, where advocacy could be applauded in theory but punished in practice.

She wanted to do more than just "support" Alex. She wanted to stand beside her, to ensure her name was respected, her presence celebrated, her future made possible. But she also knew the cost—how quickly a principal could be labeled "too political," how swiftly a single parent complaint could spiral into a school board meeting.

That's the paradox of visibility: to truly see someone, you have to be willing to be seen yourself. And that's where the risk—and the possibility—lives.

After Alex's vulnerability in the roll call, schools might shrug and move on—but history tells a different story. In the summer of 2023, high school students across the country organized under the ACLU's National Advocacy Institute to fight for trans justice. As ACLU intern Kiran Yeh reflected, "I learned how to organize with and for my trans siblings," describing the power of intergenerational organizing to protect the right to live authentically (Yeh, 2023). Their advocacy underscores a truth often missed in policy debates: visibility is not spectacle. It is a declaration of selfhood and a demand for the structural conditions that make selfhood safe.

This truth rings through media, too. The FX show *Pose* wasn't just a television series—it was cultural architecture. As executive producer Janet Mock explained, "Seeing trans folk on television . . . is the first step to people realizing that . . . we exist" (Villareal, 2018). With the largest cast of trans actors ever assembled for a scripted series, *Pose* transformed visibility into a form of historical reclamation, showing that the humanity of trans and queer people—especially Black and Latinx women—could not be reduced to background roles (Villareal, 2018). These representations affirm that when visibility is created by and for trans communities, it functions as both survival and resistance.

Similarly, the Queer Youth Assemble's List of Demands offers an unapologetic blueprint for change, calling for inclusive curricula, affirming spaces, gender-neutral facilities, pronoun recognition in school records, and access to mental health supports designed for LGBTQIA+ youth (Queer Youth Assemble, 2023). These demands are not "extras" or "accommodations"—they are educational essentials. From youth-led advocacy to cultural storytelling to policy design, visibility is the connective tissue. It ensures that students like Alex are not merely "seen" but are structurally supported to thrive.

Visibility as Liberation

To be visible—as queer, as trans, as a young person of color—is both sacred and dangerous. It is a declaration and a dare. For LGBTQIA+ youth, especially those navigating schools and systems that were never designed for their flourishing, visibility is not about being noticed—it is about being known. It is not simply about being acknowledged—it is about being affirmed. In the BRAVE framework, this is *visibility* in action: showing up as your full self and being met with the structures, policies, and relationships that sustain you.

But presence carries risk. Across the United States and around the globe, we are witnessing a deliberate assault on the visibility of queer and trans communities—particularly youth. From book bans and bathroom bills to pronoun policies and data suppression, visibility is under siege. According to an NPR investigation, entire sections of federal websites referencing LGBTQIA+ diversity were quietly removed without explanation, creating a chilling precedent for what—and who—gets erased in public life (Stone & Simmons-Duffin, 2025). The Williams Institute has also documented a dangerous rollback in access to federal data about sexual orientation and gender identity, making queer lives harder to count and easier to ignore (Conron, 2022). This erasure is not accidental. It is systemic—and it is directly at odds with the advocacy and respect pillars of BRAVE.

When data vanishes, when inclusive language is banned from classrooms, when curriculum is scrubbed of queer and trans histories, the result is not neutrality—it is harm. It is a message whispered and screamed at the same time: *You do not matter here. You are not real. You are not safe.*

Reagan, whose courage we first saw in Chapter 2, knows this feeling well. They had been misnamed more times than they could count—each moment a tiny unraveling. But something shifted the day Ms. O'Malley paused mid-sentence, corrected herself, and said their name—their name—with care and clarity.

"I used to feel like I had to shrink," Reagan later told Mr. Morales, whose classroom had become a sanctuary. "But the first time someone used my name in class—my real name—I felt like I could breathe. Like maybe I didn't have to be afraid here."

That breath—that exhale—is what visibility in the BRAVE framework makes possible. It is the moment a child's shoulders soften because they don't have to fight for recognition. It is the moment visibility becomes not a threat but a promise of belonging, respect, and advocacy—all in the same breath.

This chapter opens with a guiding question that lives at the heart of justice-centered education: What does it mean to be seen and safe—fully and freely—in the spaces where we learn, teach, and lead?

In the pages that follow, we will explore visibility as both resistance and reclamation. We will examine how art, music, storytelling, and collective action have long served as sacred vehicles for claiming space. We'll lift up the movements that made us possible, the voices that refuse to be silenced, and the creative expressions that dare to defy erasure.

Visibility is not just about showing up. It's about refusing to disappear.

Legacy Movements That Made Visibility Nonnegotiable

Visibility, for LGBTQIA+ youth of color, is not a modern convenience—it is a hard-won inheritance. To understand the urgency of being seen and affirmed today, we must look to the lineage of movements that made queer, trans, and racialized lives unignorable in the first place. These were not moments of shallow inclusion; they were declarations of humanity carved into the fabric of culture, protest, and survival. In the BRAVE framework, visibility does not exist in isolation—it is sustained by respect, advocacy, and belonging. Each of the following movements transformed the margins into the main stage, sometimes subtly, sometimes with fire.

The Harlem Renaissance (1918–1930s)

In the shadow of segregation and systemic racism, Harlem emerged as a sanctuary of cultural brilliance—a place where art became both refuge and resistance. Queer Black artists such as Langston Hughes, Countee Cullen, Alain Locke, Bessie Smith, and Gladys Bentley embedded queerness into their craft, often in coded ways that those "in the life" could recognize. Hughes's poetry blurred the lines between affection, longing, and masculinity, while Bentley—dressed in tuxedos and performing in Harlem's speakeasies—defied gender norms with unapologetic swagger.

Their art was not just personal expression; it was a survival strategy. In an era when public acknowledgment of queer identity could mean arrest, exile, or worse, their work became a subtle archive of truth. As Hartman (2020) observes, they were "making a way out of no way," cultivating visibility in plain sight while living in a society determined to erase them. The Harlem Renaissance thus stands as both cultural milestone and blueprint, showing how creativity can anchor visibility when safety is uncertain.

The Combahee River Collective (1974–1980)

Born out of the frustrations with white feminism and Black nationalism's exclusion of queer identities, the Combahee River Collective emerged as a radical Black feminist and lesbian collective based in Boston. Their foundational 1977 statement articulated, perhaps for the first time in modern political history, how interlocking systems of oppression—racism, sexism, classism, and heterosexism—demanded an intersectional analysis and an intersectional movement. They declared, "We believe that the most profound and potentially most radical politics come directly out of our own identity" (Combahee River Collective, 1977).

Visibility here was not a request; it was a strategy of survival. The Combahee River Collective gave language to a layered existence—Black, queer, woman—and insisted that liberation must be whole or it is nothing at all.

The Stonewall Uprising (1969)

June 28, 1969. After yet another police raid on the Stonewall Inn in New York City, a crowd refused to back down. Among them were trans women of color—Marsha P. Johnson and Sylvia Rivera—who resisted the brutal enforcement of gender norms and state-sanctioned erasure. Their courage ignited several nights of protest and ultimately sparked the modern LGBTQIA+ rights movement.

Stonewall was not polished activism. It was resistance born from exhaustion, grief, and rage. And it was deeply intersectional, even if mainstream narratives later tried to sanitize or whitewash it. The very bodies that were most policed—Black and Brown trans women, sex workers, drag queens, and unhoused youth—were the ones who stood first and stayed longest.

Marsha's famous phrase "No pride for some of us without liberation for all of us" remains a call to re-center visibility on those still fighting for recognition in our movements today.

ACT UP (AIDS Coalition to Unleash Power) (1987-present)

As the AIDS crisis ravaged queer communities and the U.S. government responded with neglect and silence, a new form of protest emerged—bold, theatrical, unignorable. ACT UP fused art and activism with public disruption: die-ins in cathedrals, giant pink triangles on the lawn of the White House, and slogans like "SILENCE = DEATH" plastered across major cities (Burk, 2015).

Their work forced media outlets, health officials, and the public to reckon with the faces of a crisis they tried to ignore. ACT UP's brilliance was not just in its radical demands but in its refusal to allow the dead to be buried without remembrance. In their banners, murals, and bodies chained to buildings, they made the invisible visible—again and again.

Black Lives Matter (2013-present)

Co-founded by three Black queer women—Alicia Garza, Patrisse Cullors, and Opal Tometi—Black Lives Matter radically redefined justice as driven by care, dignity, and intersectionality. That leadership lineage is not incidental: as Keeanga-Yamahtta Taylor (2020) argues in *The New Yorker,* Black feminist organizing—particularly the work of the Combahee River Collective—insisted that liberation must account for the interlocking realities of race, gender, class, and sexuality, and that coalition building only works when no one is asked to set their oppression aside for a "later" unity. In that sense, BLM's insistence on centering those most erased—Black trans women, queer activists with disabilities, and immigrant LGBTQIA+ youth—reflects a longer tradition of building movements from the ground up, rooted in lived experience and political clarity (Taylor, 2020). Their hashtags and mural art became lifelines and curriculum, coded with both purpose and resistance.

At the same time, BLM's broad visibility has been contested—sometimes reduced to symbolic alignment rather than material commitment. While scholars observe that BLM tapped deeply felt outrage rooted in the nation's unresolved history of slavery and Jim Crow (Skerry, 2021), Taylor (2020) offers a useful lens for naming the tension: when "identity politics" becomes shorthand for representation alone, movements can lose the systemic critique and collective demands that made Black feminist politics so transformative in the first place. Here, visibility shifts from mere representation to the redistribution of power, voice, and space (Taylor, 2020).

Together, these movements tell a story; that visibility is never granted—it is claimed. And every generation of LGBTQIA+ leaders, artists, and organizers has done the work of refusing invisibility. They have painted their truths across history, leaving blueprints for us to follow and demands we must still fulfill.

Visibility Through Creative Expression

Visibility isn't always loud—but it is always intentional. In schools, on stages, in hallways, in lesson plans, visibility is crafted. It is painted. It is sung. It is danced. It is written. It is embodied. For LGBTQIA+ youth of color, creative expression is more than a talent—it's a tool for survival. In the BRAVE framework, this is *visibility as liberation*: a deliberate, courageous choice to show oneself fully, even when systems conspire to erase you.

Art tells the truth when systems lie. Art builds bridges where policies build walls. Art invites joy into places where fear often lingers.

Embodied Resistance: Art as Sanctuary and Strategy

When Reagan began sketching during lunch, it wasn't about extra credit. It was about breathing. Their sketchbook overflowed with vibrant, shifting figures—some winged, some masked, some caught mid-leap between boyhood and something beautifully undefined.

"Sometimes," Reagan told Mr. Morales, "drawing is how I remember I'm real."

Their art wasn't just creativity—it was a quiet but potent assertion: *I am here. I deserve color, movement, and story.* In this way, Reagan's drawings exemplify the BRAVE principle of belonging—making space for oneself when none is freely given.

Forms of Resistance That Breathe Life into Identity

1. Visual Arts: From murals to memorial quilts, visual art makes loss visible—and hope tangible. The AIDS Memorial Quilt, one of the largest public art projects in U.S. history, transformed grief into collective memory, refusing the invisibility imposed by silence and stigma (National AIDS Memorial, 2020). In a Bronx middle school, students designed a "Queer Futures" wall—each brick painted with affirmations, chosen names, and joyful self-portraits. "This wall is where I finally saw myself smiling back," one student shared.

2. Music and Sound: Every liberation movement has a soundtrack. On Beyoncé's album *Renaissance,* the dance floor becomes a kind of sanctuary—an offering to Black queer joy, ball culture, and familial reverence, shaped by the need to dream and find escape in a frightening moment for the world (Aniftos, 2022). As Beyoncé put it, "My intention was to create a safe place, a place without judgment" (Aniftos, 2022). In classrooms, educators can treat this kind of cultural text the same way they use protest anthems—from Nina Simone to Janelle Monáe—as literacy and history lessons, helping students notice how music carries memory, movement, and resistance across generations.

3. Performance and Ballroom: Shows like *Pose* spotlight the sacred power of ballroom culture, birthed by Black and Latine trans and queer communities as both sanctuary and stage. In one Boston charter school, a Day of Queer Expression brought poetry, voguing, original music, and drag into the open—met with cheers from peers, teachers, and families. "I'd never seen myself so celebrated," one student said.

4. Spoken Word and Poetry: Poetry offers what policy cannot: space for the whole self. Writers like Danez Smith, Ariana Brown, Erica Dawson, and Saul Williams speak with a lyric urgency that mirrors the resilience of queer youth of color. Ray, a trans 5th grader introduced earlier, once performed:

I'm not a phase. I'm not confusion.

I'm a revolution.

And I'm learning to love the sound of my own voice.

Their teacher, Ms. O'Malley, taped it inside her planner, saying, "It reminds me why I show up."

Legacy of Resistance Through Art

Across history, creative expression has been both survival and strategy—but too often, narratives of queer resistance erase Indigenous, Asian American Pacific Islander (AAPI), Muslim, and immigrant voices. This absence violates the BRAVE commitment to empathy, which demands full recognition of all identities within our movements.

Two-Spirit Resistance: The term *Two-Spirit,* reclaimed in 1990 at an Indigenous LGBTQIA+ gathering in Winnipeg, honors the presence of both masculine and feminine spirits within one person (Smith, 2010). In many pre-colonial societies, Two-Spirit people were revered as healers and vision keepers. Today, artists like Arielle Twist channel grief and sovereignty through performance and poetry, centering spiritual wholeness and kinship over spectacle.

AAPI Queer Expression: Visibility in AAPI queer communities often lives at the margins, navigating silence and layered cultural expectations. From the 2004 film *Saving Face* to the poetry of Ocean Vuong, from Leo Sheng's nuanced television portrayals to Kodo Nishimura's embodiment of monkhood and makeup, these voices resist binary thinking, merging heritage and freedom.

Muslim LGBTQIA+ Creatives: Faith and queerness are not mutually exclusive. Creatives like Fatimah Asghar, the mind behind *Brown Girls,* and Samra Habib, author of *We Have Always Been Here,* speak to the fusion of religion, family, and queer becoming, reminding us that God is not the gatekeeper of love—we are.

Ballroom, Diaspora, and Sacred Joy: Ballroom houses like LaBeija and Xtravaganza remain sacred hubs of mentorship, artistry, and kinship for youth rejected by blood families (Bailey, 2013). More than performance spaces, they are chosen families with rules, rituals, and roles that nurture resilience and skill. In these circles, young people learn not only how to walk a category but how to walk into the world with pride, precision, and purpose. *Pose* brought this culture to mainstream audiences, but for many queer and trans youth of color, ballroom is not just history—it's home. Balls offer a stage where gender expression is celebrated, creativity is currency, and joy is a form of defiance.

Educator Practices for Cultivating Visibility in School Spaces

In every classroom, hallway, Zoom screen, and staff meeting, visibility either expands or shrinks. For LGBTQIA+ youth of color, especially those in conservative or politically charged environments, adult action (or inaction) signals whether they belong.

Visibility isn't just about *what* is included in curriculum or posters—it's about *who* is reflected, *how* they are named, and *why* they are centered. For educators, visibility begins in everyday choices:

- Whose names do we pronounce with care?
- Whose family structures do we acknowledge in our examples?
- Whose safety is prioritized in our policies?
- Whose joy is made possible through our pedagogy?

These questions are not neutral. They are political and spiritual and deeply tied to student well-being.

Mr. Morales: Creating a Canvas of Visibility

In his art class, Mr. Morales once observed Reagan humming under their breath while sketching—an original melody that danced between hip-hop rhythms and something almost choral. "You sing when you draw?" he asked. "Always," Reagan replied. "It helps the story come out."

Recognizing a deeper current of self-expression, Mr. Morales invited Reagan to co-lead a lesson on sound and movement in visual storytelling. He played Beyoncé's "Break My Soul" as a warm-up, offered materials for mixed media, and asked the class, "What does freedom *look* like when you can't use words?"

This was visibility through pedagogy—where students became creators, not just consumers. Where art wasn't an elective but a mirror.

Ms. O'Malley: Holding Cultural Bridges

In her ELA class, Ms. O'Malley often struggled with how to name where queerness resided in her family, especially in a district where rainbows were quietly removed from bulletin boards. But one day, during a unit on Irish immigration, she shared a family story about her great-aunt Brigid—"the black sheep," who never married, hosted raucous salons, and was known for wearing pants and quoting Sappho.

"She wasn't 'out,'" Ms. O'Malley said, "but we all knew. And we loved her for her freedom."

A student raised their hand. "Was she gay?"

"Maybe." She smiled. "And I loved her regardless."

That story opened a door for connection, especially among queer and questioning students from religious or conservative families. Visibility doesn't always mean full disclosure. Sometimes it means sharing just enough to let someone breathe easier.

Alex: Small Acts That Made Big Impact

For Alex, the turning point wasn't a pride flag or a special unit on identity. It was a hallway interaction. A substitute teacher misgendered them in front of the class. Alex froze.

But the next day, their science teacher pulled them aside and said, "Hey, I noticed what happened yesterday. I want to make sure I always call you the right name and pronouns. Can you tell me what works best?"

That moment didn't erase the harm. But it softened the isolation. Educators don't need perfect scripts. They need presence and practice and the willingness to repair.

Reclaiming the Curriculum: Teaching for Visibility and Liberation

Traditional curriculum frameworks often silence or sanitize. They erase the legacies of Black, Brown, queer, disabled, Indigenous, Muslim, Asian, and trans people in favor of a so-called "universal" narrative rooted in whiteness, colonialism, and the gender binary. But students are hungry for something else—something real, reflective, and rooted in their truth.

Reagan, who once whispered about being "too weird" to be an artist, lit up when they read about Keith Haring's use of subway graffiti to speak out about HIV/AIDS. "He was loud with it," Reagan said. "Maybe I can be loud too."

That's the point of visibility in curriculum—not tolerance but transformation. Not tokenism but truth. And yet we know: reclaiming the curriculum is political work. In red states and conservative communities, this work carries risk. But educators have always been organizers, artists, and truth tellers. Even when curriculum maps won't allow it, your classroom walls, morning circles, and book selections still speak.

Interdisciplinary Integration Ideas: Embodying Visibility Across Content Areas

Visual Art:

- Queer history murals: Have students research LGBTQIA+ icons like Marsha P. Johnson, Sylvia Rivera, Pauli Murray, Audre Lorde, or T.C. Cannon. Paint murals or digital collages featuring their faces, stories, and impact.
- Art journals of identity: Create weekly sketchbook prompts where students reflect on parts of their identity, culture, or resistance through collage, graffiti, or digital design.

Music and Social Studies:

- Liberation soundtracks: Use songs by Nina Simone, Janelle Monáe, Big Freedia, Beyoncé (especially from *Renaissance*), and others to analyze protest, joy, and visibility across movements.
- Ballroom as history: Map ballroom culture to civil rights history, discussing voguing as protest, and the role of houses as chosen family and survival strategy.

ELA and Literacy:

- Queer lit circles: Include authors like George M. Johnson (*All Boys Aren't Blue*), Leah Johnson (*You Should See Me in a Crown*), Kacen Callender (*Felix Ever After*), and Meredith Russo (*If I Was Your Girl*).
- Poetry and identity units: Anchor units in the voices of Danez Smith, Ocean Vuong, Andrea Gibson, Safia Elhillo, and Ariana Brown. Pair with student writing about "What does it mean to be fully seen?"

Theater and Performance:

- Scene reimagining: Encourage students to rewrite classic plays with modern, queer, culturally rooted adaptations. What would *Romeo and Juliet* look like if it was about Two-Spirit and Muslim teens in a U.S. border town?
- Visibility monologues: Invite students to write monologues from the point of view of someone who has been erased—or powerfully seen—for the first time.

STEM and Technology:

- Design justice projects: Have students create prototypes or tech solutions that center the needs of LGBTQIA+ youth of color. Consider apps for safety, platforms for storytelling, or accessibility tools.
- Data and disparities: Analyze reports from the Williams Institute or GLSEN on disparities in mental health, school safety, and access to healthcare for LGBTQIA+ students. Ask, "What stories do these numbers tell?"

Rituals of Affirmation and Joy:

- Affirmation walls: Designate space in your room where students display their names, pronouns, creative work, and affirmations. Update it monthly with student input.
- Dress-as-your-hero days: Invite students to dress as historical, artistic, or fictional figures who reflect their identities. Expand beyond binary and Eurocentric norms.
- Visibility week: Partner with student leaders or GSAs to host a week of celebration, storytelling, and learning. Include performances, panels, resource fairs, and history exhibits.

Tools for Educators and Leaders: Building Brave Curriculum

Curriculum is one of the most powerful tools we have for making visibility real. It shapes whose histories are told, whose identities are affirmed, and whose contributions are remembered. When curriculum reflects the fullness of LGBTQIA+ lives—especially those of Black, Brown, Indigenous, and other marginalized youth—it signals to students that they belong in the story of learning itself.

The following resources offer lesson plans, inclusive texts, professional development, and community-based projects that embed visibility into the daily life of a school. Whether you're just beginning or deeply rooted in this work, these tools can help you transform curriculum from a neutral framework into a living, liberatory practice.

- Massachusetts Commission on LGBTQ Youth Safe Schools Program (www.mass.gov/info-details/safe-schools-program-for-lgbtq-students) offers PD, anti-bullying policies, and curriculum support across K–12 schools in Massachusetts.
- Welcoming Schools (Human Rights Campaign; www.welcomingschools.org) offers lesson plans, inclusive read-alouds, and family engagement tools for K–6 educators.
- GLSEN Educator Resources (www.glsen.org/educators) offers research-based guidance on creating safe and affirming learning environments.
- Teaching Tolerance (now Learning for Justice; www.learningforjustice.org) includes the *Queer America* podcast and LGBTQIA+-inclusive lesson plans across content areas.
- Reclaiming the Native Truth Project (www.firstnations.org) uplifts Indigenous voices, including Two-Spirit perspectives, through curriculum and advocacy.

Student-Led Projects and Community Events

Creating spaces where students lead the way transforms visibility from an abstract concept into a lived, embodied experience. These projects work best when they are tied to what students are already exploring in the classroom—turning learning into action and community impact.

- **Queer visibility showcases:** Support students in organizing open mic nights, digital art galleries, or performance pieces that explore identity, justice, and joy. Link these to curriculum units on poetry, visual art, or social justice history so students can see their academic work celebrated in public spaces.
- **Schoolwide book clubs:** Choose novels or memoirs centering LGBTQIA+ youth of color and invite students, staff, and families into multi-week dialogues. Frame discussion questions around

essential curriculum themes—such as identity, resilience, or liberation—so the conversations deepen what's happening in class.

- **Day of radical joy:** Design a schoolwide celebration where students can be fully themselves without fear—through dance, dress, food, and ritual. Connect the event to lessons on cultural traditions, music history, or community organizing so it becomes more than a party—it becomes a learning experience rooted in visibility and belonging.

For Those Teaching in High-Risk Contexts

In politically hostile or high-surveillance environments, visibility work must be both strategic and protective. Here, the curriculum becomes a tool for creating "windows" into other worlds and "mirrors" for students to see themselves—without forcing disclosure or placing them at risk.

- Use "windows and mirrors" in curriculum—texts and prompts that allow students to self-reflect or learn about others indirectly, such as studying historical figures whose identities were coded or unspoken.
- Connect with trusted networks or digital communities of practice (e.g., Teaching While Queer, QTPoC Educators of Color) for vetted lesson plans and strategies that work within your context.
- Center student voice while safeguarding anonymity through private journaling, masked performances, or closed-classroom showcases tied to curricular themes like storytelling, identity, or human rights.
- Normalize pronouns, family structures, and identity-inclusive language in daily instruction so inclusion is woven into classroom routines, not treated as an "extra."

When these strategies are rooted in the curriculum—not just in isolated events—they send a powerful message: visibility is not a one-time occurrence; it is a sustained practice of respect, advocacy, and belonging.

Closing Reflections: Visibility as Sacred Practice

Visibility is not a trend. It is not a lesson plan. It is not a month of celebration.

True, embodied, liberatory visibility is sacred. It is survival. It is strategy. It is spiritual resistance.

In this chapter, we've moved through history, culture, artistry, and lived experience. We've seen how Reagan's drawings and melodies, Alex's poem, and Ms. O'Malley's family story became doorways to connection. We've watched Mr. Morales turn pedagogy into a practice of honoring, not just instructing. And we've followed educators across the country and globe, resisting erasure not through fanfare, but through fierce daily intention.

We've also faced the truth: visibility is dangerous and still necessary—especially now, in an era of coordinated erasure and violent political rhetoric. Especially when queer terminology disappears from federal websites and school districts ban history, identity, and joy (Stone & Simmons-Duffin, 2025).

In this context, visibility is not optional. It is a moral responsibility.

Being BRAVE with visibility might look like

- Designing curriculum where LGBTQIA+ lives are woven into every subject, all year.
- Publicly affirming a student's identity when it's safe—and protecting it fiercely when it's not.
- Using art, music, and storytelling as tools for both expression and survival.
- Making invisible histories visible through rituals, displays, and community celebrations.
- Modeling authentic selfhood so students know it's possible to thrive as their full selves.

BRAVE Reflection Questions

Use these in staff meetings, journaling, or advisory spaces:

- **Belonging:** What cultural rituals or creative expressions in your school affirm that students and staff can be fully themselves?
- **Respect:** When was the last time you publicly affirmed someone's identity in your classroom? What made it feel safe—or unsafe—to do so?
- **Advocacy:** Who is most invisible in your setting? How can you center their voices in your curriculum, hallway visuals, or classroom rituals?

- **Visibility:** What parts of yourself have you kept hidden in your professional role? What would it mean to bring your full self—authentically, strategically—into your practice?
- **Empathy:** Think of a student you once overlooked, misunderstood, or avoided. What visibility would they have needed to thrive?

Chapter 6 Playlist

Visit www.ccmeducationgroup.co to explore

- *Pose, Noah's Ark, Renaissance,* and other curated clips for classroom use.
- Podcasts: *The Read, Gender Reveal, Queering Desi, The Two-Spirit Conversations Project.*
- Digital quilt template for student storytelling.
- Toolkits from GLSEN, The Trevor Project, and Queer Youth Assemble.

7

Leading with Empathy and Humanity

"You get to exhale now, Simon. You get to be more you than you've been in a very long time."
—*Love, Simon* (2018)

Waiting to Exhale

There is a moment in the film *Love, Simon* that stops time. After months of internal struggle and a coming out that wasn't on his terms, Simon sits in his bedroom, unsure of what will happen next. He braces. He waits. His mother enters the room and kneels beside him. She doesn't cry right away—but you can see in her eyes that something is shifting. And then she says what so many queer youth dream of hearing:

"You get to exhale now."

It's not a dramatic monologue. It's not fireworks. It's simply a mother letting her son know: *I see you. And I still choose you.*

That moment lingers—because it reminds us of the gravity that comes with telling the truth. The exhale that only comes after surviving a world of silence, shame, and second-guessing.

Reagan watched *Love, Simon* alone on their phone one night, headphones in, blankets pulled tight. When the scene unfolded, they paused the film and just . . . stared. The longing was familiar. The vulnerability. The ache.

They hadn't yet come out to their parents. Not fully. Not in words. Their art had hinted at it—fluid bodies in their sketchbook, characters that shimmered across the gender spectrum—but nothing had been spoken aloud.

"I want to believe I could have a moment like that," Reagan once whispered to Mr. Morales. "But what if the truth makes things worse?"

Alex had already crossed that threshold. They'd come out the year before. The silence that followed from their father wasn't cruel—but it was crushing. It was the kind of silence that pretended to be neutral while quietly shifting the ground beneath their feet. "I love you" became more mechanical. "Be careful" came more often. "Let's not talk about that right now" arrived like clockwork.

Still, Alex didn't regret coming out. "I needed to say it out loud to stay whole," they said. "But I think part of me still hopes he'll come around. That one day, I'll get my *'you get to exhale now'* moment."

These are the quiet battles queer and trans youth fight long before walking through school doors. Before they sit in your classroom. Before they trust a teacher enough to ask for their correct name to be honored.

They are negotiating truth and safety in every room they enter.

To come out—to anyone—is not a simple act. It is a risk, a calculation, a sacred offering of self.

And for too many, it is met with silence, rejection, or worse.

As educators, as leaders, as caregivers, we are often not the first person a student thinks of when deciding whether to share their truth. But we are almost always *witnesses* to what follows. We see the slumped shoulders, the sharpened edge of sarcasm, the need for chosen family. We see the questions behind their eyes, asking us—without words—"Will I still be safe if I show up fully?"

And that is the question that should anchor our leadership: What does it mean to create spaces where students can exhale—fully and freely—because they know they are loved, not in spite of who they are but because of it?

This chapter is not just about school policies or inclusive posters. It is about posture. It is about how we lead with empathy and humanity, especially when silence feels safer than speaking and visibility still carries risk.

It begins with listening. It deepens with believing.

And it transforms with love that affirms: "You get to exhale now."

Empathy in Educational Spaces: Benefits and Challenges

Empathy—the capacity to understand, share, and respond to the feelings of others—is not just an emotional reflex but a pedagogical necessity. In school communities, empathy functions in four interrelated ways: as a personal trait, an emotional state, a communication skill, and a relational tool for connection (Gunn & Clark, 2022). When teachers intentionally cultivate empathy through their words, actions, and presence, classrooms become psychologically safer and more emotionally responsive. A Stanford-led study found that training educators in empathy-building strategies such as active listening and perspective-taking led to a 50 percent reduction in suspensions and marked improvements in racial equity outcomes across participating schools (Gunn & Clark, 2022).

Yet empathy is not without complexity. Neuroscientists like Jean Decety caution that emotional empathy—the raw, affective mirroring of another's pain—can lead to over-identification with those most like us (in-group bias) while unintentionally marginalizing others (Wagaman et al., 2022). In contrast, cognitive empathy, rooted in perspective taking and moral reasoning, offers a more equitable foundation for relational care and classroom justice. Schools must be intentional in how they scaffold both kinds of empathy, ensuring that they lead to action, not overwhelm or paralysis.

Empathy is not abstract—it's a daily decision that can determine whether a child feels safe, seen, and supported. For LGBTQIA+ youth of color, empathy from adults is not just about being kind—it's about disrupting silence, correcting harm, and cultivating radical presence. According to the Trevor Project (2024c), more than 40 percent of LGBTQIA+ youth seriously considered suicide in the past year, with trans and nonbinary youth experiencing the highest rates. Youth who reported having at least one affirming adult in their life—especially a teacher—were significantly less likely to attempt suicide. Empathy, in this context, is not simply affective. It is lifesaving.

Growing Empathy—and What That Means for Teens

Contrary to media narratives that frame today's youth as apathetic or self-absorbed, research reveals that empathy among adolescents is actually increasing. A national survey by the Trevor Project (2024c) affirms that LGBTQIA+ youth—especially those who engage in digital activism and mutual aid—report high levels of empathic concern and social awareness, often rooted in their lived experiences with marginalization.

Middle schoolers, in particular, offer us insight into how empathy is learned through emotional safety and guided reflection. A 2024 University of Virginia study found that students who regularly participated in discussions about ethical dilemmas, identity, and inclusion developed deeper, more internalized forms of compassion compared to those in more lecture-based classrooms (Pfister et al., 2025). These findings affirm that dialogue, not just content, is critical for empathy development.

Empathy Is Learned—and Legacies Matter

Empathy is not only teachable—it's transmissible across generations. A longitudinal study from the University of Virginia showed that adolescents whose mothers demonstrated empathic behavior during early teen years were more likely to become emotionally supportive friends, partners, and future caregivers themselves (Wagaman et al., 2022). Emotional modeling by caregivers and teachers isn't simply about the moment—it seeds a lifelong framework for relational resilience.

In school contexts, emotionally responsive classrooms translate to stronger peer relationships and academic engagement (American Public Health Association, 2024). This echoes what LGBTQIA+ youth have long known: being seen, heard, and understood changes everything.

Teaching Empathy Is Possible—and Necessary

Empathy isn't a gift; it's a learnable practice. When embedded into curricula and classroom rituals, empathy builds community and lowers behavioral challenges. Programs like Roots of Empathy, which introduce infants and their caregivers into classrooms as empathy "teachers," show sustained reductions in aggression and increases in prosocial behavior even years after the intervention (Wagaman et al., 2022). Denmark's national empathy curriculum, which begins in preschool, links emotional literacy to improved cooperation and student well-being (Gunn & Clark, 2022).

In the United States, CASEL frameworks provide a blueprint for teaching empathy in a way that advances equity. These programs move beyond kindness or politeness to include structural awareness and culturally sustaining practices—ensuring that the "who" and "why" behind empathy aren't ignored (Gunn & Clark, 2022).

Empathy Under Strain: Compassion Fatigue and Emotional Burnout

While empathy is essential, it's not infinite—especially for educators operating in high-stress, under-resourced, or politically contentious environments. When unchecked, empathy-based stress or compassion fatigue can lead to burnout, emotional numbing, or disengagement (Wagaman et al., 2022). Teachers, especially those supporting LGBTQIA+ students in states where anti-trans or "Don't Say Gay" policies are in effect, may feel the moral weight of advocacy without systemic support.

Research from PMC emphasizes the importance of compassionate responding—a framework that centers self-care, professional boundaries, and access to community for sustaining emotionally demanding work (Wagaman et al., 2022). Restorative justice, wellness check-ins, and educator peer circles are not luxuries—they are survival mechanisms in the emotional labor of justice-based teaching.

Tiered Strategies for Growing Empathy from Toddler to Teen

Empathy doesn't arrive fully formed. It must be nurtured over time—deliberately, developmentally, and with deep awareness of context. From morning meetings in kindergarten to advisory sessions in high school, empathy-building opportunities are woven through the rhythms of a school day. When educators intentionally scaffold these moments—through storytelling, reflective dialogue, and relational rituals—young people begin to internalize the belief that their emotions matter and that others' experiences deserve attention and care.

The journey of empathy growth is developmental—what works in early childhood looks very different from what resonates in middle or high school. Educators can intentionally scaffold these skills over time, moving from emotional literacy to perspective taking to empathy as leadership. The progression in Figure 7.1 illustrates how empathy can be nurtured across the school years.

For toddlers and early elementary students, empathy begins with emotional literacy: naming and recognizing feelings in themselves and others. Programs like Roots of Empathy demonstrate the power of early modeling. In these classrooms, a parent brings in their infant for regular visits, and students are guided by trained facilitators to observe the baby's emotional cues. What does the baby feel? How do we know? What would help them feel better? Over time, children learn not only to identify emotions but also to respond with compassion and problem solving (Wagaman et al., 2022). This embodied practice builds a foundation for relational awareness—long before a student encounters complex social dilemmas.

In elementary schools, storytelling and perspective taking become vital tools. Picture books that center diverse identities—like *Julian Is a Mermaid* by Jessica Love or *When Aidan Became a Brother* by Kyle Lukoff—invite students to step into another person's world. Morning meetings can incorporate "feelings circles," where students share highs and lows from their day, fostering empathy through listening. These practices are especially important for LGBTQIA+ students, who may not yet have the language to express their full identities but who long to be understood and affirmed in subtle, everyday ways.

FIGURE 7.1

Developmental Staircase for Growing Empathy

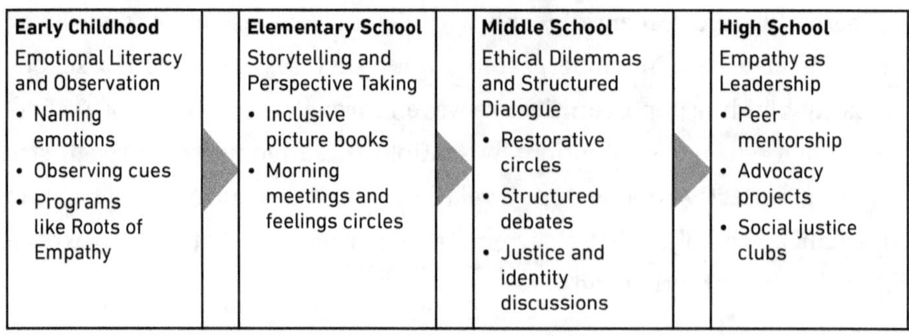

By middle school, students are developmentally ready for more nuanced conversations about justice, identity, and emotional complexity. Researchers at the University of Virginia emphasize that this age group benefits most from environments that allow them to wrestle with ethical dilemmas and emotionally loaded scenarios (Pfister et al., 2025). Advisory periods and restorative circles are key spaces to explore questions: What does it mean to stand up for someone? When is silence harmful? How can we show empathy even when we disagree?

One effective middle school strategy involves structured debates or Socratic seminars, where students are required to argue from a viewpoint different from their own. These exercises, when facilitated with care, can strengthen cognitive empathy—the ability to take another's perspective without defensiveness or harm. Teachers must create guardrails to ensure these spaces are not weaponized against marginalized students, especially those who are LGBTQIA+. But when done well, they offer young people a toolkit for compassion rooted in critical thinking.

In high school, empathy becomes a call to action. Students can reflect on their own values, beliefs, and responsibilities to community. Social justice clubs, student-led assemblies, peer mentorship, and art-based campaigns allow youth to express empathy through leadership. High schoolers also benefit from opportunities to mentor younger students, passing down relational tools and affirming their own emotional growth. SEL-aligned advisory programs that include identity exploration, trauma-informed care, and collaborative problem solving show the strongest outcomes in terms of school climate and student well-being (American Public Health Association, 2024).

Athletics and extracurricular spaces must also be recognized as key sites of empathy building. Coaches, club leaders, and faculty advisors often spend more time with students than classroom teachers. When these adults model emotional honesty and offer culturally responsive support, they extend empathy into the full fabric of school life. Imagine a basketball coach who pauses practice to check in with a player who seems emotionally withdrawn, or a drama teacher who weaves LGBTQIA+ affirming stories into script selections and casting decisions. These choices shape how students internalize empathy—not just as a concept but as a culture.

And finally, we cannot forget the role of families. Parent–teacher conferences, family nights, and digital communication platforms should not solely focus on academic performance. They are also spaces to reinforce the emotional and relational climate of the school. Schools that model empathy with families—especially with queer caregivers or families of trans and gender-expansive children—create conditions for mutual trust and collective care. Partnering with families in empathy-building practices means inviting them not just to observe but also to co-create the culture of the school community.

Building empathy from toddler to teen requires more than curriculum alignment. It requires adults who are willing to do the heart work of slowing down, listening deeply, and affirming students in all their complexity. In doing so, we create the kind of schools where young people not only succeed academically but grow into the kind of human beings who know how to love, lead, and live with courage.

Restorative Practices, Indigenous Frameworks, and Ubuntu as Community-Centered Empathy

Empathy is not just an individual skill—it is a community practice.

In many Indigenous, African, and diasporic cultures, care is not privatized, nor is conflict isolated to individuals. Harm is seen as a breach in the relational web of the community, and healing requires collective responsibility. Restorative practices, now gaining traction in schools across the United States, draw from these deep-rooted traditions. But to truly embody their spirit, we must understand their origins—not just as tools to reduce suspensions but as worldviews grounded in interconnection.

One such worldview is Ubuntu, a Southern African philosophy meaning, "I am because we are." Ubuntu teaches that our humanity is tied to the humanity of others—that each person's well-being is bound up in the well-being of the collective. When applied to education, Ubuntu becomes more than a concept—it becomes a practice of centering students' full selves, repairing relationships when harm occurs, and restoring dignity rather than assigning blame (see Figure 7.2).

Mr. Morales, a middle school teacher introduced earlier in this book, often described his classroom as a "circle, not a triangle." Every week, stu-

FIGURE 7.2
Ubuntu and Restorative Principles

dents gathered in a physical circle—knees touching, eyes level—to share stories, reflect on challenges, and affirm one another's efforts. When a student lashed out or harmed a peer, the response wasn't zero-tolerance discipline—it was a restorative conversation. Who was affected? What led to the harm? What's needed to repair the trust? It wasn't always easy, and it wasn't always clean. But over time, it taught students like Reagan and Alex that they could be both accountable and beloved.

Research backs this. Studies in urban school districts show that restorative justice practices significantly decrease racial disparities in suspension rates while increasing students' sense of belonging and connection to their school community (Smith et. al., 2025). These practices are especially impactful for LGBTQIA+ youth, who are disproportionately disciplined for "defiance," dress code violations, or perceived noncompliance—often rooted in adult discomfort rather than student behavior.

Restorative practices are not new. Indigenous nations across the Americas have long held peacemaking circles and truth-telling ceremonies as part of their community governance. These traditions center the voice of the person harmed while also honoring the humanity of the person who caused harm. They assume people can change—and that relationships are worth healing.

In many Native Hawaiian schools, the principle of hoʻoponopono—a practice of setting things right through dialogue and reconciliation—is embedded into daily interactions. Elders and cultural practitioners guide youth through processes that connect emotion, ancestry, and accountability. This isn't just discipline reform—it's cultural restoration.

In Afro-Caribbean and African American contexts, call-and-response, testimony, and communal ritual also serve as tools of emotional healing. In these traditions, empathy is not silent. It is loud, embodied, and rooted in shared rhythm. Think of a church testimony where someone shares their truth and the community responds with "Amen," "You're not alone," or "We got you." That is Ubuntu. That is restorative empathy.

Schools can learn from these models—not by appropriating them but by partnering with culture bearers, elders, and community leaders to embed them with fidelity. For instance, a school might invite a Two-Spirit elder to guide circle practices for queer Indigenous youth. Or they could partner with Black mental health practitioners to facilitate healing circles in the aftermath of community violence or policy harm.

Restorative justice is not a checklist. It is a commitment to relational repair, especially for those who have been historically silenced, criminalized, or erased. When we center empathy through Indigenous and ancestral frameworks, we resist the carceral logics that have shaped so many school systems. We move from punishment to purpose. From exclusion to re-inclusion.

In the words of Desmond Tutu, one of the foremost global champions of Ubuntu: "My humanity is bound up in yours, for we can only be human together."

Partnering with Parents: Empathy in the Family-School Bridge

Empathy doesn't begin and end at the classroom door. For many LGBTQIA+ youth, the most powerful—or most painful—responses to their identities happen at home. And educators are often caught in the delicate space between honoring a student's truth and navigating the varied beliefs, fears, and frameworks of their caregivers.

Reagan once described their coming out as "like walking off a cliff, hoping someone catches you." When they told their parents they were non-binary, the room went quiet. Their father stared at the floor. Their mother exhaled sharply. No one spoke for what felt like forever. And yet—eventually—both parents began to ask questions, clumsily but lovingly. "What does that mean for your future?" "Do you still want us to call you our daughter?" "Are you safe at school?"

It wasn't perfect. It wasn't immediate. But it was love doing its best to catch up.

Simon's story in *Love, Simon* echoes this same emotional calculus. In the moment after he comes out to his parents, time seems to slow. His truth—honest, hopeful, terrified—hangs in the air like a breath not yet released. And then comes the pause. Not rejection. Not anger. Just silence. The kind of silence that holds a thousand possible outcomes.

Eventually, the silence breaks. His father apologizes for the jokes, the assumptions, the blind spots. His mother, in a moment of gentle knowing, says, "You get to exhale now, Simon. You get to be more you than you have been in a very long time."

This is the bridge we must build between families and schools: one where students can breathe, fully and freely. But what does it take to build that bridge?

1. Start with Cultural Humility, Not Assumption

Every family walks in with different levels of knowledge, belief systems, and emotional readiness. It is not an educator's role to fix or "convert" a parent but rather to listen deeply, offer resources, and stand in solidarity with the student. Cultural humility means understanding that values around gender, sexuality, and mental health are deeply rooted—and that change, if it happens, often begins with trust.

A recent report by the American Public Health Association (2024) highlights that LGBTQIA+ youth thrive when both family and school environments are affirming, yet only 38 percent of LGBTQIA+ youth surveyed reported feeling supported at home. The stakes are too high for schools to wait passively.

2. Offer Ongoing, Not One-Off, Opportunities

Parent engagement can't be limited to annual Pride nights or surface-level trainings. Schools should create multiple entry points throughout the year for parents and caregivers to learn, grow, and engage—from empathy-building workshops to healing circles for families navigating identity transitions.

Programs like Welcoming Schools from the Human Rights Campaign provide comprehensive curriculum and training resources for educators and families alike. The Massachusetts Commission on LGBTQ Youth's Safe Schools Program offers regionally tailored toolkits, family conversation guides, and policy frameworks that center both student safety and caregiver education.

3. Create Space for Parent-to-Parent Learning

Sometimes, the most effective support doesn't come from a professional—it comes from another parent who's been there. Schools can create spaces for peer-led caregiver groups, where families of LGBTQIA+ youth can share stories, ask hard questions, and learn from one another. This models empathy not as a mandate but as a community muscle.

Alex's mother once said during a school-hosted caregiver panel, "I didn't get it at first. But when I heard another mom talk about her trans son's journey, I realized I wasn't alone—and neither was Alex."

This kind of relational empathy changes hearts more than any policy ever could.

4. Provide Resources That Reflect Diverse Identities

Not every family responds to the same language, tools, or stories. Offer materials in multiple languages. Share resources that reflect racial, cultural, and faith diversity. Provide books and videos that show queer joy, not just queer trauma. Equip families with real, actionable tools—not just theory.

Some recommendations:

- *The Gender Wheel* by Maya Gonzalez (for early learners and caregivers)
- *This Is a Book for Parents of Gay Kids* by Dannielle Owens-Reid and Kristin Russo
- The Trevor Project's Parent and Caregiver Guide
- Local LGBTQIA+ centers or affinity groups that offer family counseling or community events

5. Remember: Empathy Flows Both Ways

Parents, too, are often navigating grief, confusion, or fear—not because their child is queer or trans but because they were never given a roadmap. Educators must hold space for that complexity without compromising student safety. As one principal shared in a professional learning session, "Empathy doesn't mean agreeing. It means staying at the table, even when the conversation is hard. Especially then."

By creating ongoing, relational, and culturally responsive partnerships with families, educators extend the circle of care beyond the classroom. And in doing so, they help every student—like Reagan, like Alex, like Simon—feel a little more held.

Empathy as a Daily Act of Leadership

Empathy is not an accessory to leadership—it is the soil. It's what allows us to grow cultures of belonging, not just moments of inclusion. And for LGBTQIA+ youth, particularly those who are also Black, Brown, immigrant, Muslim, poor, or have disabilities, empathy is the difference between being seen and being erased.

When Reagan said, "Drawing is how I remember I'm real," they weren't just making art. They were making a claim to existence. When Alex stood up during an assembly and read a poem about revolution, they weren't asking for applause. They were asking not to be forgotten. And when Simon finally let the words spill out—"I'm gay"—he wasn't just revealing a secret. He was giving his family the chance to love him for his whole truth.

Each of these moments asks something of us too. They ask us to stay present when a student changes their name or pronouns. To say something when a colleague jokes about "boys wearing dresses." To reimagine advisory, not as another compliance block but as sacred space where emotions, stories, and community take root. To partner with families not only when it's easy—but when it's complex, messy, and uncertain. Empathy is not a singular gesture. It is not a one-time training. It is a daily act of brave leadership. And like all leadership, it's not about perfection—it's about practice.

As Ubuntu reminds us, *"I am because we are."* Our empathy is shaped not just by what we feel but by what we do with what we feel. It's in the hallway conversation, the curriculum we choose, the apology we offer, the silence we interrupt, and the story we make space for. Empathy reminds us that our students don't need us to be saviors. They need us to be witnesses, co-conspirators, and connectors—willing to build classrooms, schools, and systems that affirm not just who they are but who they are becoming.

So we ask again: How can we lead with empathy and humanity? By remembering that every student carries a story. By making sure they don't have to carry it alone.

Key Takeaways

- Empathy is a skill, not just a trait. Empathy can be taught, modeled, and strengthened across ages. It lives in both the heart and the habits of effective educators and leaders.
- Silence isn't neutral. When LGBTQIA+ youth experience rejection or invisibility, educator empathy can shift the outcome by affirming identity, interrupting harm, and cultivating spaces of trust.
- Cultural context matters. Empathy must be intersectional. Recognizing how race, religion, gender identity, immigration status, and class shape lived experience allows educators to respond with nuance and care.
- Restorative practices recenter humanity. Indigenous approaches like Ubuntu and community circles offer powerful models for healing, accountability, and relational learning.

- Partnerships with families must be brave and bold. Empathy includes listening to caregivers with curiosity and compassion—even when there's tension or disagreement. Relationships built on mutual respect foster safer learning spaces for all.

BRAVE Reflection Questions

Use these in staff meetings, journaling, or advisory spaces:

- **Belonging:** Who in my classroom or school still feels like they're on the outside looking in?
- **Respect:** How do I respond when students—or adults—misgender, stereotype, or silence others?
- **Advocacy:** Where am I being called to speak up more boldly—for students, colleagues, or families?
- **Visibility:** Whose stories are centered in my syllabus, hallway displays, school assemblies?
- **Empathy:** What are the boundaries and supports I need to sustain my empathy without burning out?

Chapter 7 Playlist

Visit www.ccmeducationgroup.co to access a curated library of tools, stories, and strategies that can help you build empathic, human-centered learning environments:

- Evidence-based research on empathy, trauma, and mental health in schools.
- Classroom-ready empathy-building tools, lessons, and reflective protocols.
- Youth and educator podcasts centering LGBTQIA+ voices and healing.
- Sample restorative practices rooted in Indigenous and community-based traditions.
- Advisory and SEL activities that cultivate empathy, identity, and connection.
- Resources for partnering with families around empathy and inclusive care.

These tools are ideal for sparking

- A staff professional learning session.
- A student-led empathy week.
- A restorative classroom reboot.
- A family circle or community event.
- A schoolwide audit of how empathy shows up (or doesn't).

PART III

SUSTAINING THE BRAVE WORK

8

How to Create BRAVE Communities in Hostile Times

"Caring for myself is not self-indulgence, it is self-preservation, and that is an act of political warfare."
—Audre Lorde

Bravery in the Face of Erasure

The word *brave* originates from the 15th-century Middle French *brave* (splendid, valiant) and the Italian *bravo* (bold, courageous). Dig deeper, and we arrive at the Latin *barbarus*—a term used to mark outsiders as wild, uncivilized, and threatening to the status quo.

Bravery, then, has always been about defiance. About embodying the very thing society calls *too much* and refusing to hide it. In that light, queer and trans students, teachers, and families are the most radical bearers of bravery today—not because they choose hardship but because they choose to be visible in a world that tells them not to be.

To truly understand the urgency of this moment, one must pause—not just to read the headlines but to feel what it means to be legislated out of existence. Not metaphorically, not abstractly, but literally.

Imagine this: you are a 14-year-old trans girl in Arkansas. You've just started feeling safe enough to wear your hair the way you like. You've started to smile in photos again. Your mom drives 90 miles every other week for you to meet with a therapist who listens without judgment and helps you believe that your life is worth living. Your school counselor updates your records quietly. Your English teacher pulls you aside to say how proud she is. And for a moment—just a moment—you begin to believe you belong.

Then one morning, you wake up to the news that everything supporting your survival is now illegal.

This isn't hypothetical. It's unfolding right now under the shadow of Project 2025 (Heritage Foundation, 2023)—a sweeping, ultraconservative agenda crafted by the Heritage Foundation and backed by powerful political figures. This isn't a backroom conversation. It's a publicly available, 900-plus-page manifesto designed to overhaul federal policy and roll back decades of civil rights protections—particularly those safeguarding LGBTQIA+ people, educators, and students.

The plan includes

- Title IX reinterpretation: Redefining sex-based discrimination to exclude gender identity. This would legally allow schools to misgender students, deny access to restrooms or sports, and ban trans-inclusive policies altogether.
- Defunding DEI: Eliminating diversity, equity, and inclusion programs across all federal agencies, including those that protect students from race-based or sexuality-based harassment.
- Parental rights expansion: Forcing educators to disclose a student's gender identity to parents, even when that disclosure could put the student at risk of harm or homelessness.
- Federal agency overhaul: Dismantling the Office for Civil Rights and the U.S. Department of Education—stripping marginalized students of any federal protection if state and local systems fail them.

For many LGBTQIA+ students, school is the only place where they are affirmed. These policies weaponize that space—turning it into a surveillance zone instead of a sanctuary.

Supreme Court Ruling: Criminalizing Care, Criminalizing Love

In June 2025, the U.S. Supreme Court upheld Tennessee's ban on gender-affirming medical care for minors in the landmark case *United States v. Skrmetti.* The decision, decided 6–3 along ideological lines, sets a dangerous precedent that other states are now following. In the majority opinion, Chief Justice Roberts wrote, "Our role is not 'to judge the wisdom, fairness, or logic' of the law . . . but only to ensure that it does not violate the equal protection guarantee of the Fourteenth Amendment. Having concluded it does not, we leave questions regarding its policy to the people, their elected representatives, and the democratic process" (Roberts, 2025). The Court determined that Tennessee's law hinges on age and medical classification—not sex or gender identity—and therefore only warrants rational basis review, the most lenient standard of judicial scrutiny.

Justice Sotomayor, in her dissent, strongly challenged the majority's logic: "The majority subjects a law that plainly discriminates on the basis of sex to mere rational-basis review. By retreating from meaningful judicial review exactly where it matters most, the Court abandons transgender children and their families to political whims" (Fields, 2025). "This ruling invites untold harm to transgender children and the parents and families who love them." Her language makes clear that this isn't just a legal theory—it is a collective moral failure.

The Court's decision immediately transforms the lives of transgender youth and their supporters:

- Puberty blockers, hormone therapy, and surgical interventions are now criminalized in states with similar bans—even for youth previously approved by licensed providers.
- Parents face legal scrutiny. In Tennessee, Ohio, Nebraska, and elsewhere, families can be investigated—and even prosecuted—by Child Protective Services for allowing their child to live authentically.
- Medical professionals risk criminal charges. Despite consensus from the American Academy of Pediatrics, American Psychological Association, and Endocrine Society about the safety and necessity of gender-affirming care, doctors and mental health providers now face potential jail time (Burga, 2025b).

Impact Across States: Red and Blue Realities

The American promise of equality feels increasingly fractured for LGBTQIA+ students, their families, and the educators who support them. Across dozens of states, hostile legislation and judicial rulings have reshaped the day-to-day experiences of young queer and trans people—not in abstract terms but in very real ways: name changes denied, health care criminalized, and teachers forced into silence.

The Red State Reality

In Tennessee, the Supreme Court's 2025 decision to uphold a statewide ban on gender-affirming care set off a wave of similar legislation across red states (Roberts, 2025). States like Ohio and Nebraska quickly introduced laws criminalizing medical professionals and parents who support transgender minors. In Texas, existing restrictions have escalated to include penalties for teachers who use a student's chosen pronouns without explicit parental consent (Human Rights Campaign, 2024a). These laws are framed as "parental rights" protections, but in practice, they have become mechanisms for surveillance and punishment—targeting the most vulnerable.

In conservative states, legislation has shifted from codified prejudice to empowered erasure. These laws aren't abstract policy—they are lived experiences shaping daily decisions.

Healthcare bans and forced outing:

- South Carolina's H.B. 4624, signed in May 2024, bans puberty blockers, hormones, and gender-affirming surgeries for minors. It also forces school staff to notify parents if a student uses pronouns or a name inconsistent with their birth-assigned sex. Providers face felony charges for offering care to minors (ACLU, 2025).
- Wyoming, Tennessee, Missouri, Kansas, New Hampshire, and others enacted similar bans—criminalizing gender-affirming medical care and penalizing supportive providers or parents (ACLU, 2025).

Censorship and "Don't Say Gay" laws:

- States like Florida, Alabama, Iowa, Montana, North Carolina, and Texas enacted laws restricting classroom instruction about

LGBTQIA+ identities, banning pronoun discussions, and institutionalizing parental opt-out requirements (ACLU, 2025; Movement Advancement Project, 2024).

Bathroom and sports bans:

- Nearly 75 percent of trans youth live in states with bans on restroom access consistent with their gender identity, sports exclusion, or pending legislation to restrict visibility (Conron, 2022).

These laws directly harm youth through forced invisibility, legal vulnerability, educational sabotage, and mental health crises. Teachers are silenced, parents fear losing custody, and counselors are banned from affirming identity. Research shows LGBTQIA+ youth in these states feel unsafe, erased, or censored—and educators report removing LGBTQIA+ content to avoid legal risk (ACLU, 2025)

Human Costs in Red States: Real Stories of Survival and Advocacy

For students, the impact is swift and punishing. A 14-year-old in Arkansas was removed from their home after a teacher reported the child's transition to Child Protective Services. In Florida, a high school junior was forced to return to their birth name on school records despite a suicide attempt the previous year linked to gender dysphoria. Educators in these regions face impossible ethical crossroads. Some go silent to protect their jobs. Others risk termination to affirm a child's existence with something as simple as a sticker on their laptop that says, "You are loved."

The fear isn't paranoia. It's policy.

Laws in at least 23 states now explicitly prohibit educators from discussing gender identity or sexual orientation in classrooms, even as part of anti-bullying or civil rights lessons (Movement Advancement Project, 2024). These "Don't Say Gay" and "Curriculum Transparency" policies have expanded beyond early grades, reaching high school and even teacher preparation programs. Teachers caught in the crossfire are resigning, relocating, or resisting quietly—creating underground networks of lesson sharing and emotional support (Bozard, 2023).

- In Missouri, parents must survive delays of 18 months and up to 15 evaluations before their child can begin treatment—despite medical consensus on care protocols. Many families face financial ruin or flee the state to access services (ACLU, 2025).

- In Kansas, transgender high school athletes—and even middle schoolers—have lost opportunities for inclusion, affecting scholarships, community acceptance, and identity affirmation (ACLU, 2025).

Educators in Blue States: Holding Space Under Pressure

Meanwhile, in blue states, leaders are actively working to counteract the damage. Massachusetts, California, and Illinois have passed legislation codifying gender-affirming care as a protected right for minors and adults, including access within public schools and state-funded health centers (GLSEN, 2024). New York City schools have implemented districtwide LGBTQIA+ training programs for staff, while the San Francisco Unified School District offers wellness centers that provide confidential support for students, regardless of their family's acceptance.

While red states legislate erasure, progressive states and sanctuary states try to build protective frameworks rooted in care and resistance.

Shield laws and sanctuary policies:

- Maine, Rhode Island, New York, Oregon, New Jersey, Washington State, and Colorado enacted laws explicitly protecting gender-affirming care as a fundamental right, and they refuse to cooperate with out-of-state enforcement (ACLU, 2025).
- Delaware became a 2025 sanctuary state, banning civil or criminal cooperation on out-of-state care restrictions and protecting provider data (ACLU, 2025).

Outing protections and family privacy:

- California's AB 1955, signed in July 2024, prohibits schools from forcing educators to notify parents when a student self-identifies as LGBTQIA+ and shields teachers from discipline over inclusive discussions (Modan, 2024).

Inclusive curriculum and public celebration of identity:

- States including New York, California, and Washington have enacted LGBTQIA+-inclusive curricular standards. Around 25 percent of LGBTQIA+ youth live in states where queer histories and identities are required in social studies, literature, or civics curricula (Movement Advancement Project, 2024).

Even in sanctuary states, educators report tension. In reality, policies exist on paper but experiences differ:

- Some California districts still push out staff over speaking about LGBTQIA+ identities; teachers use coded language to protect students (Smallens, 2024).
- Legal challenges persist—as DOJ threats and subpoena campaigns continue targeting clinics in New York, Massachusetts, California, and Illinois (Mulvihill, 2025).

Living Between Two Worlds

Still, the pain does not end at state borders. A student from Alabama who relocates to Connecticut for safety still carries trauma, mistrust, and grief. A teacher from Oklahoma may find sanctuary in Oregon but will likely leave behind their pension, home, and a school community they loved. As the country bifurcates into havens and hazards, the mental health toll becomes staggering.

The Trevor Project's (2023b) national survey found that 39 percent of LGBTQIA+ youth seriously considered suicide in the past year, with the rate rising to 54 percent among transgender and nonbinary youth. Those in states with restrictive laws were 38 percent more likely to experience depression or anxiety compared to peers in affirming environments. The American Psychological Association (2024) echoes this, noting that even the discussion of anti-LGBTQIA+ laws creates measurable harm, particularly in youth who internalize messages of shame and disposability.

We are living in an unequal America—one where a child's right to dignity is determined by ZIP code. Yet even in the shadow of such disparities, brave educators, families, and youth are organizing, storytelling, and resisting. In conservative towns, librarians host banned book clubs. In progressive districts, students raise funds for peers navigating unsafe homes. And in both places, love—quiet and loud—persists.

Because even when policy fails, the community can still rise:

- For cisgender, white educators in red states: Your silence upholds the system. Your identity grants invisibility to others. When you speak or shield, discipleship shifts.
- For youth in blue states: Solidarity across lines matters. Your art, your advocacy, your stories sustain the impossible hope of those in restrictive states.
- For families: Sanctuary states offer legal safety. But real sanctuary isn't just a law—it's a community that believes your child deserves care, protection, joy.

This national tapestry—of hostility, resistance, and sanctuary—makes clear that bravery isn't optional. It's relational. It travels through networks of teachers, advocates, siblings, clinics, artists, and faith leaders, refusing erasure.

Visible and Unapologetic: BRAVE Movements for Our Time

In every corner of the United States—from bustling cities to small rural towns—LGBTQIA+ communities are organizing, creating, and resisting in ways that defy erasure. These movements do not emerge in isolation; they are forged in response to legislative attacks, cultural stigmatization, and systemic inequities. Whether in the form of mass mobilizations, creative policy workarounds, community-based Pride events, or large-scale public art installations, each act is a refusal to accept a future defined by fear. Together, they weave a living record of resilience, proving that the fight for liberation is as much about joy and connection as it is about protest and policy change.

No Kings Protests: Boston, MA

On June 14, 2025, Boston's streets became both a parade route and a protest line. Under drizzling skies, marchers twirled rainbow umbrellas, waved pride flags, and set off from Copley Square for a route that wound through the Back Bay, uniting the annual Pride celebration with the "No Kings" demonstrations taking place across the country (Guerra, 2025).

Organizers were intentional about the convergence. Boston Pride for the People's theme, "Here to Stay," carried a clear message: LGBTQIA+ people will not be erased, silenced, or pushed into the shadows amid escalating political attacks. As the crowd moved, the energy shifted seamlessly between celebration and defiance—joyful cheers paired with pointed chants against authoritarianism and discrimination.

For some attendees, their very presence was political. "I'm a gay Latino immigrant and a U.S. citizen, and I am proud of the way that my life has gone and the intersectionality of all of my identities," said Brian Gonzalez, 37, of Boston, holding a Mexican pride flag. "And being me means sticking it to the man, and that's why I'm here" (Guerra, 2025).

Others came to protest specific rollbacks under the Trump administration. "I'm here because the administration is removing protections for the LGBTQ community in federal housing and federal contracts—essentially eliminating the right for trans people to exist," said Marianne Voss, 54, who traveled from Connecticut with her 17-year-old daughter, Maya. For 81-year-old Jeffrey Margulies of Roslindale, the protest's name held personal resonance: "We don't want a king. We want our government to care for us, not to put us down" (Guerra, 2025).

The event's sponsors—including Mass 50501 and Indivisible Mass Coalition—called on attendees to "dance, sing, and resist, with Pride." At a City Hall pride flag raising earlier that month, Boston Mayor Michelle Wu underscored the stakes:

> When we say Boston is a home for everyone, that means ensuring there are spaces where courage isn't required to survive. Where being yourself doesn't demand being brave all the time. It means less time building resilience and more time building joy.... None of it can be taken for granted. (Guerra, 2025)

Jean Dolin, CEO of the Boston LGBTQ+ Museum of Art, History and Culture, reframed the narrative away from deficit: "Yes, we are under attack. Yes, we are a traumatized community, but we're also hella strong. We get a lot of things done and we contribute a lot" (Guerra, 2025).

No Kings Day in Boston made that strength visible—turning the city into a living reminder that Pride was, and remains, born from protest. It was both a declaration and a celebration: a refusal to be erased and an insistence on joy as resistance.

World Pride Rally: Washington, DC

On a rain-splashed Sunday morning at the Lincoln Memorial, hundreds gathered for the closing rally and march of WorldPride 2025. The crowd erupted in cheers when former Vice President Kamala Harris appeared on stage screens, delivering a surprise message:

> Pride is about honoring the trailblazers who came before, joining arms with those leading the fight for equality today, and empowering the next generation to live boldly, freely and with joy. . . . No one should be made to fight alone. We are all in this together. (Shammas et al., 2025)

For three weeks, WorldPride transformed DC into a festival of drag performances, dance parties, activist talks, historical exhibits, and concerts—all underpinned by the belief that visibility is power. Hundreds of thousands traveled from across the United States and around the world to be present (Shammas et al., 2025).

For many attendees, the moment was deeply political. South Florida visitors Mitch Pizik, 63, his partner Jay Abbit, 44, and their friend Lester Wild, 66, wore T-shirts styled like Tide detergent, reading, "Pride: Removes stubborn orange stains." Abbit explained:

> Often when fascism starts to rise, queer people are the first targets. . . . So it's important that we make a stand together, we're visible together, and we show the world our strength together. (Shammas et al., 2025)

Over 100 participants from a morning National Trans Visibility March—who joined in chanting "When I say, 'trans liberation,' you say, 'now'"—infused the rally with additional momentum. Among them was Datoria Hobson, a Black trans woman, who said that while they were prepared for safety issues, the reception had been unexpectedly affirming. Her friend, Bellamy Douglas, 26, from Atlanta, added:

I haven't always been feeling part of the community, so seeing this was inspiring. We're walking not only with ourselves but with all of our trans sisters. We're out here together." (Shammas et al., 2025)

As the march began, signs bobbed above the crowd reading "Trans people will always exist" and "Gay is good." WorldPride's final act was equal parts celebration and resistance—affirming that, despite political backsliding, the LGBTQIA+ community remains visible, unified, and unwavering.

Clark County's First Pride: La Center, WA

In a quiet, rural enclave, Clark County Pride is a big deal. La Center, Washington—a southwest town of 4,300 without a single stoplight, only three restaurants, and no hotels—might seem an unlikely setting for one of the region's most joyful acts of resistance. Yet each year, the annual parade and festival transforms its modest downtown into a hub of celebration and solidarity.

When Clark County Pride first marched in 2021, just 100 people braved record-breaking 100-degree heat to attend. Organizers installed five cooling tents, stocked with water stations and misters, along the 0.9-mile route, and some participants joined from the comfort of air-conditioned vehicles. In the years since, attendance has ballooned to nearly 700 people, along with dozens of vendors whose food, drinks, rainbow flags, and handmade jewelry make the festival their single most profitable day of the year.

The event's origins were urgent and personal. The first Pride was pulled together on short notice after organizers learned LGBTQIA+ students at local middle and high schools were being bullied. In a town this small, Plaugher says, Pride is often the only opportunity queer youth have to "find their people" and feel less alone. She recalls one moment from last year: an 8th grader approaching her to say quietly, "I made my very first friend today" (Deml & Salk, 2025).

"It's become so big and loud—in the joyful, happy way," Plaugher said. "To folks who are ignorant of what it looks like to celebrate Pride and what the meaning of it is, I would like to see them be unable to deny the fact that we are safe, happy, and courageous. I would like the naysayers to be unable to deny the positive impacts that our community has on the area."

For Clark County, Pride is more than a parade—it is proof that, even in the most rural corners of the country, joy and courage can outshine prejudice. It is a day where community is visible, voices are amplified, and no one has to wonder whether they belong (Deml & Salk, 2025).

Freedom to Be Monument: Washington, DC

On May 17, 2025, the National Mall became a patchwork of resistance and joy. The Freedom to Be Monument, a 9,000-square-foot quilt installation composed of 258 panels made by transgender people and allies, stretched less than a mile from the White House—where the Trump administration has sought to roll back transgender rights (Uber, 2025).

Each quilt told a story. One panel read, "Life, Liberty, and the pursuit of Happiness for trans Idahoans." Another, decorated with floral patterns and the transgender flag, pleaded for the right not to be forced into a binary on a South Dakota driver's license. A third, from Kansas, declared, "I define my existence, and I exist defiantly."

The American Civil Liberties Union, which is challenging Tennessee's ban on gender-affirming care for minors at the Supreme Court, had sent quilting kits across the country with a single prompt: "What does freedom mean to me?" One panel from the ACLU of Kansas, featuring a stick-figure family, answered: "We want the freedom to live here. Trans people often flee rural areas for opportunity and safety. Freedom to be, to us, means the freedom to slay—to stay and still be able to keep ourselves and our family safe" (Uber, 2025).

As one speaker put it,

> It's easy to get lost in the rhetoric of those frightened by our freedom—talk of bathrooms or sports or lies about our health care. But here's the thing—what terrifies them the most is our joy. That's what it is, and that's what this is. These quilts, this art, all of us here: this is a testament to our joy. Today is a protest, but in true queer fashion, it is also a party, darling. (Uber, 2025)

The rally traded chants for live music, and DJ sets under stage signs proclaiming "Trans Joy Is Protest." Peppermint, the ACLU's Artist Ambassador, reminded the crowd that this act of creation was rooted in history: "Let's take a moment to remember that we are not the first to stitch resistance into fabric." The installation launched the first day of WorldPride, an international LGBTQIA+ festival drawing millions to Washington, DC, at a time when transgender rights in the United States face unprecedented legislative threats. Here, joy and protest were not opposites—they were inseparable threads in the same fabric of survival.

Salt Lake City's Banner Strategy: Salt Lake City, UT

On the eve of Utah's new pride flag ban, Salt Lake City leaders moved with precision and purpose. Hours before the law took effect, the City Council unanimously adopted three new official city flags—each featuring the city's white sego lily emblem but infused with unmistakable meaning: one in the rainbow colors of the LGBTQIA+ flag; one in the light blue, pink, and white stripes of the transgender flag; and one with the bursting star of the Juneteenth flag (Cabrera, 2025).

Mayor Erin Mendenhall framed the move as both lawful and deeply principled: "I know that the values of diversity, equity, and inclusion are not only right and just, but they are fundamental to America, even through all its struggles to uphold them."

By designating these banners as official municipal symbols, Salt Lake City found a legal pathway around HB77—a law banning nearly all flags in government buildings except those on a narrow, state-approved list. The law, signed without Governor Spencer Cox's signature, was championed by conservative legislators who called the city's maneuver "political theatrics" and a "waste of taxpayer resources."

For City Council member Darin Mano, however, the decision was about more than policy—it was about place:

> This is the place where people like us feel safe . . . and so this is important and critical for us as a city, but more importantly for the people that live here to know that Salt Lake City continues to be a safe space for everybody. (Cabrera, 2025)

Critics in the state legislature, including the bill's sponsors, quickly mocked the decision online. But inside City Hall, the mood was resolute. Council member Victoria Petro challenged residents to focus on priorities beyond political culture wars.

Mendenhall acknowledged the city's long history of clashing with Utah's Republican-majority legislature but said the goal was to represent Salt Lake City's values—not provoke: "My intent is to represent our city's values and honor our dear diverse residents who make up this beautiful city and the legacy of pain and progress that they have endured."

Across the state line in Idaho, Boise's City Council followed suit, adopting the pride banner as an official city flag—signaling that, in some cities, the response to restriction will be more visibility, not less.

State-Level Resistance: Maine in the Crosshairs

In February 2025, at a National Governors Association event at the White House, President Trump confronted Maine governor Janet Mills over her state's refusal to comply with his executive order banning transgender athletes from girls' sports teams. When Trump warned that federal funding could be cut, Mills stood firm: "We're going to follow the law, sir. We'll see you in court." Trump shot back, "Good. I'll see you in court . . . and enjoy your life after governor, because I don't think you'll be in elected politics." Mills later reaffirmed the state's resistance: "The State of Maine will not be intimidated by the President's threats" (Schapitl, 2025; McCauley, 2025; Bose & Chiacu, 2025).

That defiance led to mounting federal pressure. The Department of Education initiated a Title IX investigation, and the USDA temporarily froze over $2 million in school nutrition funding. But Maine fought back in court—and won. By May, the USDA agreed to unfreeze the funds, an outcome Governor Mills called "a victory . . . we did see him in court, and we won" (Levin, 2025; Riedel, 2025).

This high-stakes showdown highlights how state-level leadership can transform into a powerful act of resistance. When armed with integrity and legal resolve, solidarity becomes more than symbolic—it becomes unignorable.

These movements and acts of resistance demonstrate that bravery is not a singular gesture—it is a collective, ongoing commitment to visibility, equity, and justice. From the streets of Boston to the small-town parks of Clark County, from the halls of state government in Maine to the symbolic banners flying over Salt Lake City, communities are refusing to be legislated out of existence. They remind us that resistance can be celebratory and fierce, rooted in love as much as in defiance. And they challenge us, as educators, leaders, and allies, to recognize that every rally, proclamation, art installation, and Pride event is not only a moment of courage but also an invitation: to join, to protect, and to carry the work forward.

Activating Your BRAVE Superpowers

Regardless of whether you teach in a state with anti-LGBTQIA+ policies or one with affirming legislation, you have the power—and responsibility—to cultivate belonging and protect your students' humanity. Below are practical, research-backed strategies that educators across the country can implement to support LGBTQIA+ youth, challenge harmful narratives, and build resilient school communities.

Belonging: Create spaces where students feel rooted.

- Build classroom rituals that affirm identity (e.g., "name of the day" intros, art that reflects diverse identities, identity journaling).
- Use trauma-informed practices to check in on emotional safety. A daily mood meter or anonymous note box gives students a voice.
- Integrate inclusive classroom libraries with LGBTQIA+ authors and characters, even if you avoid explicitly labeling them in hostile climates (Bozard, 2023).

Respect: Honor names, pronouns, and boundaries.

- Use chosen names and pronouns privately even if you cannot affirm them publicly due to legal restrictions.
- Create private intake forms at the start of the year (or semester) for students to share their pronouns, access needs, and comfort levels.
- Avoid outing students under any circumstances. Let students lead their identity disclosures and respect their pace and privacy.

Advocacy: Practice quiet or loud resistance.

- Know your district's policies on student records, classroom discussion guidelines, and what's protected under FERPA or Title IX—even in restrictive areas.
- Teach resistance through history by highlighting diverse civil rights leaders without naming sexuality explicitly (when needed).

- Use student-led projects to amplify marginalized voices through research, oral histories, or community interviews that center social justice.

Visibility: Signal safety subtly or publicly.

- Wear subtle symbols of support like a rainbow lapel pin, bracelet, or sticker. In less affirming schools, these signals speak volumes.
- Display inclusive posters or quotes that don't use LGBTQIA+-specific language but still reflect affirming values (e.g., "All Students Welcome Here").
- Collaborate with your art or ELA department to display student-created work about identity, community, or family.

Empathy: Foster dialogue, not debate.

- Use restorative circles or community agreements to open dialogue about identity and belonging in age-appropriate ways.
- Teach empathy skills explicitly through books, films, and media (e.g., the perspective-taking approach used in Roots of Empathy programs).
- Model emotional literacy by narrating your own learning, making space for others' stories, and holding space for discomfort.

Bonus: Professional Courage Moves

Regardless of where you're located, *you* deserve support too. Brave educators need brave ecosystems.

- Join national educator networks like GLSEN, NEA's LGBTQ+ Caucus, or the Human Rights Campaign's Welcoming Schools Program.
- Create an underground coalition of affirming educators in your school or district. Share resources, provide emotional support, and offer classroom walkthroughs.
- Start a community care calendar to check in with one another regularly—especially after local policy changes or political flare-ups.

Resilience Practices in Hostile Climates

When the air feels heavy with hostility, survival requires intentional care. In restrictive states, educators and students alike are finding ways to breathe, connect, and hold onto themselves:

- **Affinity moments:** Carving out five minutes before or after class for queer and allied students to check in, share a word of encouragement, or swap art and music (GLSEN, 2024).
- **Code-switching for safety:** For many BIPOC and queer or trans students, classrooms can feel like spaces where visibility comes with real risks. This practice involves using affirming language, symbols, or imagery in ways that signal belonging and support—without always explicitly labeling LGBTQIA+ identity. It creates subtle, culturally aware entry points for safety and affirmation so students can see themselves reflected without fear of being outed or targeted (Lambda Legal, 2024).
- **Storytelling rituals:** Using anonymous journaling prompts that invite students to reflect on courage, family, and hope, a practice supported in trauma-informed classroom guidelines (American Psychological Association, 2024).
- **Educator wellness anchors:** Committing to one daily act that nourishes your spirit—whether that's texting a trusted colleague, journaling gratitude, or stepping outside for sunlight between classes.

Resilience in hostile times doesn't mean pretending things aren't hard. It means building micro-sanctuaries within your day that remind you—and your students—that joy is still yours to claim.

BRAVE Together or Not at All

To create BRAVE communities in hostile times is to refuse the lie that some students are disposable. It is to teach with our backs straight and our hearts open, even when fear claws at the door. It is to build a sanctuary in classrooms, courage in our conversations, and a community beyond policy. While anti-LGBTQIA+ legislation spreads, our resistance must become more relational, more rooted, and more radical. We cannot wait for permission to protect children. We must become the teachers, leaders, caregivers, and neighbors who look at each young person and say, *You are not too much. You are not alone. You belong.* Because in the end, we are either brave together or not at all.

Key Takeaways

- Bravery is collective, not just individual. It means disrupting policies and practices that dehumanize LGBTQIA+ youth.
- Project 2025 and recent court rulings represent unprecedented legal and cultural attacks on queer and trans existence in schools.
- Gender-affirming care includes more than medical support—it also means using chosen names, affirming pronouns, and having access to culturally responsive mental health services.
- Faith communities and global allies are stepping in where U.S. policies have failed, providing models for sanctuary and solidarity.
- Educators everywhere can act, regardless of region, using universal, trauma-informed, and affirming strategies aligned with the BRAVE framework.

BRAVE Reflection Questions

Use these in staff meetings, journaling, or advisory spaces:

- **Belonging:** How do I intentionally create spaces where students feel they are seen, valued, and needed—not just accepted?
- **Respect:** In what ways do I honor students' identities through my daily language, tone, and classroom agreements—even when no one is watching?
- **Advocacy:** When have I remained silent out of fear—and what would a small, safe act of advocacy look like in my context today?
- **Visibility:** What visible cues do I offer that signal to LGBTQIA+ students that they are safe here, even in subtle ways?
- **Empathy:** How am I actively practicing empathy—not pity—for students and colleagues navigating systems designed to erase them?

Chapter 8 Playlist

Visit www.ccmeducationgroup.co to access a curated library of tools, stories, and strategies to help you build empathic, human-centered learning environments.

These tools are ideal for sparking

- Trauma-informed class check-in templates.
- LGBTQIA+-inclusive read-alouds (PreK–12).
- Sample student intake/pronoun surveys.
- Lesson plans on empathy and civil courage.
- An emergency safety plan for students experiencing home rejection.
- Advocacy letters and scripts for school board engagement.

Partnering with Parents, Caregivers, and Community Partners

"Pride starts with yourself and being proud of who you are. . . . I hope that they're proud not only of themselves but of the family that they've been born into."

—Jesse Tyler Ferguson

Centering the Light: When We See the Child First

The air was heavy with late spring humidity as Ms. Elena Thompson opened the door to her school office. The counselor, a white woman in her early 40s with kind eyes and a quiet resilience honed over two decades in public education, had scheduled the meeting for after the final bell. She liked it that way—less distraction, more time for the heart work. Today's meeting wasn't about transcripts or test scores. It was about Alex.

Alex had a 3.9 GPA, led the school's Gender and Sexuality Alliance, and had recently written a play that made three teachers cry during its first staged reading. Her gifts were undeniable, but her path to this moment had been anything but easy.

By the time she turned 12, Alex had already been marked by systems—rejected by her biological family after her mother discovered her trying on makeup and heels in their tiny bathroom. "Boys don't do that," her mother had said. "Not under my roof." And with that, she was gone—swept into the foster care system where girlhood wasn't protected, and Black trans girlhood was barely acknowledged at all.

Years of instability followed—group homes, emergency shelters, nights spent in corners of bus stations, and caseworkers who changed more frequently than her shoes. But at 14, everything shifted when she met Yvette and Caroline Moore—a married couple with a warmth that softened Alex's defenses almost immediately.

Yvette, a bold, Afro-Caribbean playwright in her late 40s, had grown up with protest in her blood. Caroline, a soft-spoken white ER nurse from Vermont, had hands that knew how to stitch wounds and hold grief. Together, they gave Alex what she hadn't had in years: a home where her name was spoken with pride.

Now in her junior year, Alex was beginning to dream out loud about college. But lately, those dreams had quieted. Ms. Thompson noticed it during advisory—Alex had begun missing sessions about college applications and skipping the mentoring program she once led with enthusiasm.

When the Moores arrived, Yvette's gold bangles clinked as she hugged Ms. Thompson warmly. Caroline offered a grateful smile, her eyes weary from a 12-hour shift. They took seats beside the window where sunlight cast soft patterns across the carpet.

"I wanted to check in about Alex," Ms. Thompson began gently, her tone steady but warm. "Her grades are still excellent, and her teachers are singing her praises. But something's shifted. She's pulling back."

Yvette nodded. "She told us she doesn't think she's going to get into any of the schools she wants. Said she's not what they're looking for."

"She said she's too complicated," Caroline added, voice tight with emotion. "Too political, too queer, too . . . everything."

Ms. Thompson felt her throat catch. "She's afraid they'll Google her, see that she's trans, see her essays about identity and foster care, and decide she's too much." She paused. "And I get it. The world still punishes brilliance in bodies like hers."

Yvette's eyes flashed. "We told her we're not chasing schools that need her to dilute herself. We want spaces that can handle her light. That can hold it."

"Exactly," Ms. Thompson said. "I've been compiling a list of colleges with strong LGBTQIA+ support systems, ones that offer scholarships for foster youth and have student wellness centers that walk the walk." She leaned forward. "I'd love to build her a college plan that affirms who she is—not one that makes her beg to be accepted."

Caroline reached across the table, touching Ms. Thompson's hand. "That means the world. She listens to you. And she needs to see this kind of support—especially from someone in a system that hasn't always protected her."

Ms. Thompson blinked back tears. "She is one of the most extraordinary young people I've ever met. Her story isn't a liability. It's her legacy."

Yvette smiled. "Let's build something bold. She's never had a soft place to land—until now. Let's make sure she knows she's already enough."

And in that small room, with the hum of the school's air conditioning whispering in the background, three adults locked arms around one radiant girl. No application deadline, no admissions committee, and no hostile policy could take that away.

Closing Reflection

Alex's story is not just one of resilience—it is a reflection of what becomes possible when educators and families coauthor futures grounded in radical care. Too often, LGBTQIA+ youth are seen through the lens of risk rather than brilliance. But when we listen deeply, when we center the conversation on a child's light rather than their labels, we begin to transform the systems that failed them.

This chapter is an invitation to you to be an advocate who sees past the fear and into the fire. Be the one who says, "You are not too much. You are exactly what this world needs."

Why Partnership Matters for Belonging and Safety

Earlier in this book, we explored what it means to create classrooms and school cultures that are BRAVE—spaces rooted in belonging, respect, advocacy, visibility, and empathy. But even the most affirming teacher, counselor, or principal cannot do this work alone. Brave belonging is not just a pedagogical practice; it is a community commitment. It cannot thrive in isolation.

In Chapter 3, we unpacked what belonging looks like when embedded in daily school life. In Chapter 7, we explored how empathy must be practiced across all layers of a child's world—from advisory periods to morning meetings to restorative justice circles. And in Chapter 8, we named the hostile realities facing LGBTQIA+ youth: from the criminalization of gender-affirming care to the dismantling of protections once guaranteed under Title IX.

What these stories and strategies reveal, over and over again, is this truth: When families and communities are aligned with schools, protective factors multiply. When they are not, youth are left to navigate violence, confusion, and shame—often alone.

A BRAVE classroom matters. But what happens when that classroom is tucked inside a school where leadership is silent, or where district policies reinforce harm? And even when a school is affirming, what happens when a student goes home to rejection or enters a community where visibility equals danger?

This is the tension that so many young people—especially Black, Brown, queer, trans, and immigrant youth and those with disabilities—live in daily. They may thrive inside school hallways, only to shrink back into silence at home or in their neighborhoods. Some find refuge online. Others disappear into invisibility as a means of survival. The stakes could not be clearer.

Across national and international studies, one theme consistently emerges: youth do best when school, home, and community environments are all affirming.

- LGBTQIA+ youth who had at least one accepting adult were 40 percent less likely to report a suicide attempt in the past year (The Trevor Project, 2024c).
- School connectedness is a powerful protective factor, but its impact doubles when students also feel safe and supported at home and in their community (CDC, 2023).
- A meta-analysis on LGBTQIA+ mental health revealed that intersectional support systems (including community centers, faith spaces, and athletic programs) reduce depression and anxiety in

queer and trans youth by as much as 60 percent (American Psychological Association, 2024).

Put simply, bravery is most sustainable when it's scaffolded. When a school commits to inclusion but a student's home life remains hostile, educators become emergency responders rather than long-term partners. And when families are supportive but school environments remain rigid or exclusionary, students are forced to compartmentalize their identities. But when we build ecosystems of safety, we reduce the pressure on individual actors—teachers, social workers, or parents—and instead weave a collective net of protection, affirmation, and love.

Building Constellations of Collective Care

When we widen the circle of care beyond school walls, we begin to see what it truly means to cocreate brave communities. While educators are often on the front lines, it is community partners—local organizations, families, and informal networks—who help carry the weight and extend the reach of belonging.

For Alex, our Black transgender student introduced earlier, it was not just her affirming school counselor or her 3.9 GPA that kept her grounded. It was also the gentle presence of her foster mothers—Yvette and Caroline—who helped her rehearse her college essay out loud in the living room. It was the LGBTQIA+ youth center director who told her she could wear her heels and hoodie and still be enough. It was the free community legal clinic that helped her update her records and the faith-based counselor who told her, "You are already whole."

These relationships formed a constellation of care, making it possible for Alex to dream—not just survive.

The Power of Parent and Community Partnerships with Schools

BRAVE communities don't materialize from a single institution or policy shift. They are intentionally woven from the threads of many different sectors—schools, homes, churches, clinics, art spaces, and grassroots organizations. To build communities that truly honor and protect LGBTQIA+ youth, we must think beyond school walls. We must look to our partners—often overlooked, sometimes under-resourced, but always essential.

Youth centers and after-school programs are often the first places where young people begin to explore who they are, free from the academic pressures and hierarchical structures of the school day. These spaces offer a level of flexibility and relational closeness that classrooms sometimes cannot. When staff are trained in trauma-informed practices, gender inclusivity, and cultural humility, these environments become sacred ground—where young people can try on pieces of themselves, test their voice, and learn they are not alone. When schools partner with these centers to cohost LGBTQIA+ youth nights or college readiness workshops that center trans and queer youth, they signal something powerful: "We see you. We're showing up, even when it's after hours" (Human Rights Campaign, n.d.).

In the realm of sports and recreation, belonging looks different. Identity formation happens here too—on the field, in the locker room, and through team chants and shared struggle. Yet these spaces can be exclusionary for trans, nonbinary, and gender-expansive youth (Kean, 2020). Rigid gender norms and outdated policies around uniforms or bathrooms send a clear, harmful message: *You can play, but only if you hide.* Some districts have begun to rewrite these norms, bringing coaches into professional learning sessions about equity and inclusion, reimagining what a "team" truly means (National Education Association, n.d.). In doing so, they open space for every youth—regardless of gender expression—to compete, collaborate, and thrive.

Faith communities present a more complex but equally important opportunity. For many LGBTQIA+ youth and families, religion has been a source of shame, silence, or violence. And yet, it is also in these communities that many find their most transformative healing. Inclusive congregations—particularly those led by Black, Brown, queer, and progressive clergy—are modeling a different kind of sacred belonging. They are hosting gender-affirming name ceremonies, welcoming GSAs into fellowship halls, and preaching from pulpits that affirm the divine spark in every child (PFLAG, n.d.). When schools build interfaith coalitions that uplift these spaces, they offer students something rare and holy: spiritual safety.

Health and mental health providers are another essential part of the care web. For youth navigating trauma, dysphoria, and chronic stress, access to gender-affirming and culturally responsive care can be lifesaving. School–community partnerships with clinics like Fenway Health, Planned Parenthood, or Black-led therapy collectives can bring those services closer to where students already are. Whether through onsite counseling, telehealth offerings, or staff training to reduce harm, these partnerships expand the definition of school safety to include psychological and physical well-being (Young, 2025).

Meanwhile, arts and cultural organizations remain underutilized allies in this work. These are often the spaces where queer and trans youth first feel seen—not just tolerated but celebrated. In murals, in poems, in dance, young people articulate truths that defy language. Schools that partner with museums, theaters, and youth-led art collectives to showcase student voices aren't just offering extracurricular activities. They're making a declaration: *Your story belongs here.*

For youth in foster care, those disconnected from biological family, or those who exist in the liminal spaces of chosen kinship, family is not always defined by blood. In many cases, a mentor, a coach, a neighbor, or a foster parent becomes the anchor. Schools that create space for these nontraditional caregivers—through storytelling nights, caregiver advocacy circles, or home-school codesign teams—shift the conversation from behavior management to identity celebration (Human Rights Campaign, n.d.). They understand that family engagement must be redefined in ways that reflect lived reality, not institutional assumptions.

And in the age of book bans and curriculum erasure, libraries and bookstores have emerged as unexpected battlegrounds of truth and liberation. These spaces hold history, imagination, and resistance all at once. When schools collaborate with local librarians or independent bookstore owners to host banned book clubs, queer author panels, or storytelling nights, they protect young people's right to know themselves. They teach that censorship will not define this generation's education (National Education Association, n.d.).

What binds all of this together is not just a list of partnerships—it's a mindset. True partnership is not transactional. It is not a checklist or a photo op. It is transformational. It requires humility. It demands that we show up with curiosity, listen deeply, adjust our assumptions, and cocreate alongside those most impacted. It is forged through a shared mission, collective action, and mutual accountability.

To build these ecosystems of care is to live out the values of brave leadership. It means inviting the voices of parents who have been told their children are "too much" (PFLAG, n.d.). It means learning from faith leaders who hold both conviction and cultural nuance. And it means being bold enough to ask the hard question "Who is not at the table—and why?"

In the Orbit of Bravery: What Happens When Care Meets Conflict

It was almost dismissal when the knock came.

Ms. O'Malley looked up from her laptop, where she'd been responding to yet another email about spring assessments and staffing changes. The voice outside the door was small. Hesitant.

"Ms. O'Malley? Can I . . . can I talk to you?"

She recognized it immediately—Devon, a 5th grader she'd known since he was in 1st grade. He had that careful kind of voice some kids carry when they've already learned the cost of taking up too much space.

Ms. O'Malley smiled gently and waved him in. "Of course, kiddo. Come on."

Devon didn't sit right away. He stood by the chair, clutching the strap of his backpack like it was the only thing keeping him tethered to the floor. His eyes darted toward the window, the closed door, the wall of college pennants behind her desk.

"I've been trying to tell someone," he began, barely above a whisper. "But I don't know if it's . . . like, bad."

Ms. O'Malley froze, not visibly but enough to notice it in herself. The tremble of intuition. The weight of a moment arriving.

Devon looked at the floor. "They keep calling me gay in class. And weird. And . . . the other word. The one that rhymes with 'bag.'" He swallowed. "I don't even know if I *am*. But I can't sleep. I don't want to come to school. And I can't tell my parents because . . . they'd be so embarrassed. You know how they are with church and stuff."

Ms. O'Malley did know. She'd shared potluck plates with Devon's parents at local community events, sat beside them during town hall meetings, and even held Devon on her hip at a holiday tree lighting when he was younger. His parents were kind. Faithful. Vocal. And they had no idea that their child—10 years old, maybe just beginning to form the language for his feelings—was unraveling under the weight of shame and silence.

What Devon didn't know was that Ms. O'Malley was unraveling too.

She thanked him for sharing, promised he wasn't in trouble. He was safe with her. But even as she spoke the words, part of her was sinking beneath the surface.

Because the truth was: she wasn't sure how she felt about "the gay thing," either.

She'd grown up in a town not far from this one. Her upbringing had been steeped in Catholic guilt and coded disapproval, the kind that never used slurs but still made clear who belonged and who didn't. She'd come into adulthood thinking she was an ally—until the first time a rainbow flag appeared in the school library and she felt a flush of panic. Until a parent wrote a complaint and mentioned her name. Until a colleague asked her to sign on to a district equity statement that explicitly named LGBTQIA+ youth, and her pen hovered midair.

Now, face to face with Devon's pain, that hesitation felt like betrayal.

And yet . . . she hesitated still.

What if she supported him openly and the family pulled him from the school? What if the church families in the district turned on her, called her out at school committee meetings, labeled her the principal who was "pushing an agenda"?

What if she lost the relationships she'd spent years building?

She looked at Devon—small, tired, trying to be brave—and saw her own reflection in his doubt. She saw the cost of her silence.

But she still didn't speak.

Instead, she walked him back to class, hand gently on his shoulder. She told him she'd think about what they could do next and promised she'd check in again tomorrow.

Then she closed the office door and sat back down at her desk.

It was quiet again. But not peaceful.

Ms. O'Malley stared out the window at the school parking lot, her breath shallow, her heart louder than she wanted it to be.

She knew this wasn't over. Not for Devon. Not by a long shot.

Engaging BRAVEly Amid the Tension

Ms. O'Malley's story is not unusual—and that's exactly why it matters.

Across the country, educators are carrying the weight of secrets shared in quiet moments: a child whispering that they might be gay, a teen asking a trusted adult to use their chosen name in private, a middle schooler drawing a pride flag in the corner of their notebook and quickly erasing it when someone walks by.

These moments are sacred.

But they're also dangerous.

In states like Texas, Florida, and Alabama, educators are increasingly placed in impossible positions. Newly enacted laws require school personnel to inform parents of changes in a student's pronouns, gender identity, or participation in LGBTQIA+ programs—often without the student's consent. Failure to comply may result in job loss, license revocation, or even criminal penalties.

And yet, the emotional and psychological risk to students is just as real. The Trevor Project (2024c) found that LGBTQIA+ youth who are outed without consent are significantly more likely to experience suicidality, housing instability, and school dropout. Even well-meaning parental disclosure can rupture safety if the home environment is unsupportive or violent.

This tension—between legal obligation and moral responsibility—is not theoretical. It lives in the breath educators hold when a student says, "Can I tell you something?" It lives in every hallway conversation, every report card comment, every PTA meeting.

So how do we, as educators and leaders, navigate these moments not just carefully, but BRAVEly? The BRAVE framework (belonging, respect, advocacy, visibility, empathy) offers a roadmap for values-driven, trauma-informed, and culturally grounded action. In these high-stakes moments—especially those involving parents, caregivers, and community partners—we must activate an expanded form of it.

Engaging BRAVEly with Families and Partners

Each letter becomes a compass point for navigating the complexity with integrity.

Belonging over Binary: Lead with the conviction that every child deserves to belong, even when the world demands they choose between false binaries. When talking to caregivers, emphasize shared values: safety, love, potential. "I want your child to feel like they can succeed here—not just academically but as their full self."

Respect with Rigor: Respect doesn't mean avoiding discomfort. It means approaching every conversation with care, clarity, and the courage to uphold boundaries rooted in dignity. This includes redirecting harmful language, challenging stereotypes, and calling in caregivers who may not understand but are willing to learn.

Advocate Within and Beyond: Sometimes, the most powerful advocacy is quiet and strategic. In restrictive environments, this might look like embedding inclusive books into the library, offering anonymous support group links, or aligning with external partners (e.g., youth centers, affirming therapists) to ensure students aren't left alone. It also means helping families understand what affirming support truly looks like.

Visibility with Discernment: Visibility is a double-edged sword. For some students, being seen is lifesaving. For others, it's a risk. Ask, don't assume. "What name and pronouns would you like me to use here—and are you OK if others hear me use them?" Be mindful of documentation policies, hallway conversations, and who else is listening.

Empathy Embodied: Empathy isn't a feeling—it's a practice. It means honoring the lived reality of students *and* the fears of families, especially in communities where queerness has been demonized. It means making space for grief, confusion, and transformation.

Legal Literacy: Understand your local and state policies, but don't weaponize them. Consult legal experts, union reps, and LGBTQIA+ advocacy organizations to stay informed. In some cases, it may be legal to withhold information at a student's request. In others, documentation or FERPA laws may provide creative cover.

Youth-Centered Always: Return to the student. What do *they* need? What helps them feel safe? What role do they want you to play? Even when constrained, centering youth agency restores humanity to systems that too often strip it away.

There is no one-size-fits-all approach. Some conversations may require a pause. Others may demand bold clarity. What matters most is that educators never forget their *why*: to protect, to uplift, to liberate. For every law that threatens silence, there are thousands of educators speaking truth through practice. For every policy that aims to erase, there are constellations of care being built in classrooms, homes, community centers, and whispered affirmations between child and trusted adult.

Ahead, we return to Ms. O'Malley—and the question she must answer for herself: Will silence protect her—or betray the very child who trusts her most?

How Might You Respond BRAVEly?

These true-to-life vignettes reflect the tensions, challenges, and ethical crossroads educators face when working with LGBTQIA+ youth—particularly in a climate where affirming identities may be met with resistance, risk, or confusion. We invite you to read each scenario with intention and pause to reflect before moving to the next.

Scenario 1: Playground Whispers and the 1st Grader in Pink

A 1st grade teacher notices that Amir, a bright and expressive student, enjoys twirling in princess costumes and singing to himself on the playground. He gravitates toward creative play, often joining the girls during recess. Lately, Amir has been teased by a few boys who call him "sissy" or "weird," and the teacher notices him withdrawing more and more each day.

Reflection questions:

- What assumptions might we unconsciously make about gender expression in early childhood?
- What preventative steps could help shape a more inclusive play environment?
- How might you engage families in a conversation about classroom culture without centering fear?
- What messages—explicit or subtle—are children receiving from adults about who they're allowed to be?

Scenario 2: Hidden in the Closet—Literally

Mya, a 4th grade girl who is usually confident, talkative, and energetic, has started hiding in the back of the classroom coat closet during free reading time. After a note was discovered where Mya expressed her feelings for another female classmate, whispers and giggles followed. Her demeanor has shifted. She refuses to talk during class and often asks to go home early.

Reflection questions:

- How do we hold space for a student navigating same-gender attraction for the first time—especially in the face of peer cruelty?
- What is our role as educators when a child hasn't disclosed their feelings to family?
- How might trauma-informed practices help shape your next steps?
- What systems are (or aren't) in place to respond to harm in ways that restore dignity?

Scenario 3: "Call Me Skylar" in a Florida Classroom

In a quiet moment after class, a middle school student confides in their teacher. They say they no longer want to be called Lorenzo and instead go by Skylar. They identify as nonbinary, prefer they/them pronouns, and believe they are bisexual. Their father, who is active in the school community, has spoken publicly against "gender ideology" and supported new legislation that limits LGBTQIA+ discussion in schools.

Skylar asks the teacher not to tell anyone—not even their parents.

Reflection questions:

- What do you do when a student confides in you but the law requires you to disclose their identity to caregivers?
- How do you honor student safety while navigating professional risk or policy restrictions?
- What does bravery look like when the stakes are legally and emotionally high?
- Who might be part of your constellation of care in this moment?

Scenario 4: Sidney's Studio Breakdown

An art teacher walks into the classroom to find Sidney, a 10th grader, crying uncontrollably. A classmate has outed her by sharing screenshots of private messages with her parents. In response, Sidney's parents kicked her out of the house the night before. She hasn't slept, has no place to stay, and feels completely alone.

The teacher recalls when their own sister was forced to leave home after coming out—and that same helplessness is rising again.

Reflection questions:

- What are the first three things you would do?
- How might your own experiences shape your response—for better or worse?
- What resources, people, or policies in your school community would help you support Sidney?
- How do you emotionally prepare to witness and respond to youth in crisis?

When You Don't Know What to Say or Do: Showing Up Anyway

There are moments when your heart is in the right place but your experience, language, or confidence just hasn't caught up yet. You're not part of the LGBTQIA+ community. You've never had to come out. You've never faced bullying for your pronouns or been told your identity was a "phase." But you're here. You're reading this. You care deeply about your students. And you don't want to hurt them—not through ignorance, not through silence, and certainly not through inaction.

Still, you're afraid.

Afraid you'll say the wrong thing. Afraid you'll get a pronoun wrong. Afraid you'll make it worse by trying to make it better.

You're not alone. And you're not failing. The truth is many educators—even those with decades of experience—wrestle with the fear of "messing up" when supporting LGBTQIA+ youth. Research from the American Psychological Association (2024) and GLSEN's (2024) National School Climate Survey affirm that supportive adults, regardless of sexual or gender identity, significantly reduce the risk of depression, suicide, and school disengagement among LGBTQIA+ youth. What matters most is not perfection—it's presence.

You don't have to be part of the community to be part of the solution.

The Cost of Silence

It's not uncommon for well-meaning educators to remain quiet in moments of harm—when a student is misgendered, when slurs are whispered on the playground, or when a parent disparages gender-affirming practices.

The silence is often rooted in uncertainty, not cruelty. But for LGBTQIA+ youth, silence can feel like abandonment.

The Human Rights Campaign's (2023) LGBTQ+ Youth Report found that nearly half of LGBTQIA+ youth never hear supportive comments from teachers about their identities, and only 19 percent say they can "definitely" be themselves at school. But here's what's equally true: One affirming adult can reduce suicide risk by 40 percent (The Trevor Project, 2024c). You can be that adult.

What If I Make a Mistake?

You will. We all do.

You may misgender a student. You may forget a pronoun or use a deadname. You may stumble in a parent conversation or feel paralyzed when a student comes out.

But harm does not have to be permanent when accountability is present. Students do not expect you to be perfect. They expect you to try—and to own your mistakes with honesty and care.

Strategies to Show Up BRAVEly—Even When You're Unsure

Each of the following strategies aligns with the BRAVE framework (belonging, respect, advocacy, visibility, empathy) and is grounded in evidence-based practices and trauma-informed care.

1. Pause and Reflect—Not Retreat

Before rushing to fix or apologize, take a moment to reflect. What triggered your discomfort? Was it fear of judgment, lack of knowledge, or concern about community response? Knowing your "why" helps you lead from integrity instead of shame. Educators who engage in self-reflective practice and vulnerability-centered professional development are more likely to form authentic, affirming relationships with marginalized students.

2. Model Repair When Harm Happens

If you use the wrong name or pronoun:

- Acknowledge it quickly and calmly. "I'm sorry—I meant Skylar. Thank you for your patience."

- Don't over-apologize. Students shouldn't have to comfort you.
- Circle back privately if needed to ensure the student is OK and knows you're committed to doing better.

If you were silent when harm happened:

- Name it later. "I've been thinking about what happened yesterday. I should have spoken up when you were being laughed at. That wasn't right, and I'm sorry."
- Repair in action. Address the broader class, adjust community norms, or seek restorative dialogue.

According to a study published in *Frontiers in Psychology*, teacher modeling of accountability behaviors improves classroom trust and student perceptions of fairness, especially among marginalized populations (Wagaman et al., 2022).

3. Speak from Curiosity, Not Certainty

If you don't know how a student identifies or what language to use, ask gently and appropriately.

4. Create "Opt-In" Safety

If your context prohibits open affirmation (e.g., conservative districts, state mandates), create layered options:

- Anonymous suggestion boxes
- Gender-neutral bathrooms
- Private check-ins
- Inclusive books and posters

These gestures, while quiet, can signal safety and respect without breaching policy.

5. Partner with Those Who Know More

You don't have to do this alone. Reach out to

- Your school's GSA or LGBTQIA+ coordinator.
- Local LGBTQIA+ community centers.
- Faith leaders or parents who are affirming.
- National organizations like GLSEN, The Trevor Project, and PFLAG.

You may never know exactly what it feels like to walk in the shoes of your LGBTQIA+ students. But your role isn't to *be them*. Your role is to believe them. To affirm them. To hold space for their becoming.

Every time you choose to learn, every time you apologize with humility, every time you advocate—even imperfectly—you are helping build a world where students like Alex, Skylar, Mya, and Amir get to live without shame.

And that is brave.

Ms. O'Malley's BRAVE Return: Courage as Constellation

The morning after Devon shared his fear, Ms. O'Malley didn't have all the answers. She couldn't promise every outcome—but she could choose how to show up.

Belonging

She opened school early, leaving her office door open. Throughout the morning, she intentionally created small interactions—with Devon and others—checking in with casual warmth. Without singling him out, she reinforced that Devon's presence mattered. When he passed her in the hallway, she greeted him by name—and used the pronoun he'd shared.

Respect

Ms. O'Malley recognized her own tension: torn between loyalty to the community and compassion for her student. Rather than ignore her uncertainty, she brought it to the school culture team—expressing it not as shame but as anxiety rooted in caring. More than saying, "I'm sorry," she committed to growing alongside Devon, implicitly honoring his pace and identity without forcing exposure.

Advocacy

Instead of public statements that might provoke resistance, Ms. O'Malley took strategic steps. She quietly arranged restorative circles when teasing incidents occurred. She collaborated with the counselor to offer anonymous feedback options for students uncomfortable discussing identity topics. And she approached guiding leadership about reviewing school policies around teasing and restorative response—not as punitive measures but as teachings about respect.

Visibility

Ms. O'Malley oversaw a subtle shift in the school environment: a display of student illustrations about identity and belonging (none explicitly labeled but rich in identity symbolism). She ensured library shelves featured inclusive books. She used neutral language during announcements that included references to chosen names and pronouns—creating cues of visibility without overt signaling that might threaten Devon's privacy.

Empathy

Privately, Ms. O'Malley reflected on the history she carried: echoes of guilt and silence from her Catholic upbringing. She leaned into grief for what she hadn't known before—and allowed that grief to fuel her care, not immobilize it. When Devon looked at her tentatively at lunch, she looked back without words—and that pause communicated more than any script could.

Legal Literacy

Although the community values her, Ms. O'Malley intentionally sought guidance from the district's legal liaison and union representatives. She examined thresholds defined in state law and confirmed where discretion lay. Her actions were anchored in policy awareness: affirming when she could, conserving when necessary, and never betraying her student.

Youth-Centeredness

Every move was grounded in Devon's experience. Ms. O'Malley returned to him every afternoon—not to quiz or extract information but to hold space. She let him guide the level of disclosure he wanted, including whether he wanted a counselor or trusted ally present. When he whispered a tentative, "Thank you," she just nodded—knowing the resonance of that small word meant everything.

The Impact

Within days, Devon seemed steadier. He smiled a bit more at recess. He rejoined center activities at lunch. Teachers checked in, reporting his shift.

A conversation opened in the teacher's lounge about how to address subtle teasing in other grades. Although still fragile, Devon wasn't invisible.

Ms. O'Malley didn't save him. But she risked discomfort, potential community pushback, and personal anxiety—and in doing so, she demonstrated that courage doesn't have to be loud. It just needs to be faithful.

Her actions rippled: setting safer norms, modeling repair instead of retreat, and showing that one adult's bravery can illuminate possibilities for an entire school.

BRAVE Partnership Is the Only Way Forward

BRAVE leadership refuses to let safety stop at the classroom door. It links arms with parents, caregivers, community leaders, and affirming faith centers to ensure belonging travels with a child—into their home, their after-school space, their neighborhood, and every space in between. For Black, Brown, queer, trans, and immigrant youth, especially, this collaboration is not optional. It is the difference between isolation and affirmation, between risk and refuge. When educators work alongside families who affirm and keep the lines of communication open for those still learning, they expand the safety net beyond any one teacher, classroom, school, or policy. In a climate where laws attempt to silence, erase, dehumanize, and diminish, we cannot wait for permission to connect. We must be the educators, caregivers, community partners, neighbors, and allies who look at each young person and declare, "Your safety is not up for debate. Your brilliance is not too much. Your story belongs everywhere you go." Because, in the end, we can either choose brave partnership or leave our children to navigate these dangerous terrains alone.

Key Takeaways

- Partnership is a protective factor—when home, school, and community align, LGBTQIA+ youth are more likely to thrive.
- Caregivers and partners may be affirming, hesitant, or resistant—bravery means engaging across difference while holding firm to dignity and safety.

- Community organizations, arts spaces, youth centers, and faith communities can expand belonging beyond school walls.
- Legal literacy is essential; knowing policies protects both students and educators in high-stakes situations.
- The BRAVEly framework offers a roadmap for navigating tension with integrity and centering youth voice.

BRAVE Reflection Questions

Use these in staff meetings, journaling, or advisory spaces:

- **Belonging:** How do I extend belonging beyond the classroom into homes, neighborhoods, and community spaces?
- **Respect:** How am I showing respect to families and partners who may not yet share my understanding but are open to listening?
- **Advocacy:** When have I connected a student to an external partner to protect or affirm their identity?
- **Visibility:** What visible cues do I offer that let families and partners know this is a safe place for LGBTQIA+ youth?
- **Empathy:** How do I hold empathy for both students and caregivers when values clash—without compromising safety?

Chapter 9 Playlist

Visit www.ccmeducationgroup.co to find a curated library of tools, stories, and strategies that can help you build partnerships that protect and affirm LGBTQIA+ youth:

- Conversation starters for engaging hesitant or resistant caregivers.
- Partnership MOUs with LGBTQIA+ community organizations.
- Templates for inclusive event invitations and caregiver listening sessions.
- Legal literacy guides for educators navigating parental disclosure laws.
- Sample "constellation of care" maps for youth support planning.
- Resource lists for affirming faith communities, arts organizations, and health providers.

BRAVE Forward: The Work Is Ours Together

"If you have come here to help me, you are wasting your time. But if you have come because your liberation is bound up with mine, then let us work together."

—Lilla Watson

The Bravery I Didn't Name (But They Saw Anyway)

Some days, I wake up wondering if I'm showing up as the brave educator I write about. Other days, I know I'm not. I still wrestle with fear, with hiding, with how much of myself to bring into spaces that aren't always built for me—or for those who look, love, or live like me.

Being BRAVE is not a clean or comfortable process. It's messy, emotional, dangerous. And at its best? Liberating. It's the kind of work that can feel like a runner's high—like every cell in your body is aligned with purpose. But it can also feel like a gut punch from Mike Tyson in his prime.

My journey toward brave visibility began long before I ever had the language for it. As a Black, queer, male elementary educator who grew up in New Orleans, I spent the first decade of my career closeted—or, more accurately, very carefully concealed. I had quietly come out to a close family member here and there, maybe a trusted friend, but I lived with a constant fear that being outed would mean the end of my career.

To be Black, male, queer, and a classroom teacher in New Orleans, then Texas, then Boston . . . was some of my best life's work. But it came at a cost. I kept my personal life close to the vest, not because I was ashamed, but because I didn't feel safe. The world didn't yet offer protections for educators like me—not in policy, not in culture, not in community.

And if I'm honest, I internalized a lot of the messages I'd grown up hearing: that Black male teachers who weren't coaches or deans were "soft" or "funny acting," and teaching wasn't aspirational enough. Some of my friends in corporate America couldn't wrap their heads around why I'd pour my energy into a classroom instead of chasing six-figure bonuses. Being a teacher didn't always get me the second date.

And yet, there I was—six-foot-three, cornbread-fed, weighing in at over 260 pounds with a deep voice, a little flair for the kitchen, and a heart as big as the dreams I held for my students. Their mothers adored me. As for some of their fathers—let's just say I had a few unexpected fans there too.

But it wasn't until I facilitated a book club years later—reading either *Gender Queer* by Maia Kobabe or *Belly of the Beast* by Da'Shaun Harrison—that something shifted. One of the parents from my former school joined us. I braced myself, unsure how my queerness would land now that it was center stage in the content.

After the session, she pulled me aside and said:

> Mr. Martin, we all knew back when you was at the Hale. We saw it. We saw *you*. We loved you and didn't have an issue with it. Yeah, the parents talked. The kids talked. But it wasn't a thing—because you was about your business. You were about dem kids. And that's what mattered to us.

I froze. My heart stopped a little. Because, for the first time, I wasn't just seen. I was affirmed as a *brave educator*—by someone I'd been silently trying to protect myself from for years. And in that moment, the story I'd been carrying—the one where being out would be a liability—started to crack open.

Over time, I've had countless conversations with former students, parents, and colleagues who shared things they'd heard, said, or celebrated about me—long before I ever claimed it publicly. They told me how my authenticity inspired them, how my presence gave them permission, how my courage, even in hiding, was somehow still visible.

What I've learned is this: People often see your bravery before you do. And sometimes, the bravest thing you can do is simply keep showing up—for the children, for the community, for yourself.

Back then, I didn't want my sexuality to become a distraction. I didn't want my queerness to be weaponized against the work I loved. I didn't want parents questioning my motives or children being denied what they needed. I just wanted to teach, to lead, to serve. And yet, the deeper truth is this: There is no real "serving" without authenticity. No true leading without vulnerability. No meaningful liberation without being fully seen.

And now, I lead out loud. I teach out loud. I love out loud.

Because even if the world is still catching up, I've decided that my bravery is not up for debate.

From Awareness to Action: The Arc of the Journey

As we arrive at this final chapter, I want to remind you that this is not the conclusion of our work together. It is a turning point, a beginning. If this book has done its job, you've been called not just to think but to transform—yourself, your classroom, your community.

We've walked through the BRAVE framework—not as a linear model but as a sacred arc. We explored belonging through Reagan's quiet resilience. We reflected on respect by listening to Ray's courageous truth. We named the tension in advocacy, where imperfection and repair coexist. We witnessed visibility as protest and as prayer. And we came full circle through empathy—that sacred tether that reminds us we are not doing this work alone.

These pillars are not isolated. They are interwoven, cyclical, and sacred. They call us to act, not from perfection but from compassionate accountability. As Zaretta Hammond (2014) teaches in *Culturally Responsive Teaching and the Brain,* belonging is not a warm and fuzzy add-on—it is a neurological prerequisite for learning. And as Gholdy Muhammad (2020) reminds us in

Cultivating Genius, identity development and criticality must sit at the center of any education that claims to be transformative.

But beyond pedagogy and policy, this is soul work.

We carry the sacred responsibility of creating space for students whose light has too often been dimmed—by curriculum that erases, by leadership that punishes difference, and by silence that cloaks violence. This is the kind of work liberation psychology describes, not as individual therapy but as *collective healing.* Not as reform but as reclamation. The late Ignacio Martín-Baró, who coined the term, wrote that liberation cannot happen within the structures that created the oppression in the first place. Instead, it must emerge from new relationships of solidarity, truth-telling, and action.

That's what this book has tried to offer—a path from awareness to action. Not as a checklist but as a sacred calling.

Co-Liberation: The Future We Build Together

Let's be clear: This work is not charity. It is not saviorism. It is not diversity theater. It is co-liberation—actively knowing and living that none of us are free until all of us are free.

The term *co-liberation* demands that we center the most marginalized—not as an afterthought but as a starting point. Black queer feminist theory, from the Combahee River Collective to Audre Lorde, teaches us that we cannot dismantle oppressive systems using the same tools that built them. This means we cannot tokenize youth voices while hoarding decision-making power. We cannot demand visibility for queer students without building policies that ensure their safety. We cannot center anti-racism in our curriculum while remaining silent on anti-trans legislation. The work must be whole.

Healing and liberation don't happen through institutional change alone. They grow in community—through relationships, accountability, and the daily practices that make people feel safe, seen, and held. In other words, we move at the speed of trust.

Imagine a school in 2030—not perfect but brave.

In this school:

- Students call each other by chosen names without hesitation.
- Teachers model repair, not performance.
- Queer joy is not a risk—it is a rite.

- Coaches, clinicians, and community partners are trained not just in tolerance but in *trauma-informed affirmation.*
- The curriculum reflects every child's ancestry and agency.
- Caregivers are welcomed into the fold, not silenced by jargon or shame.

That school is not a fantasy. That school is a choice. And we build it together.

Metrics That Matter: Rethinking Success

If we want to build a co-liberated future, we must change what we measure. For generations, schools have centered metrics that monitor behavior, obedience, and achievement—often at the expense of humanity, identity, and belonging. We've obsessed over standardized test scores, suspension rates, and attendance numbers. But liberation doesn't live in a spreadsheet. It lives in how young people feel when they walk through the door.

Gloria Ladson-Billings (1995) reminds us that culturally relevant pedagogy is not just about *what* we teach but *why*. In her framework, student achievement must always be in service of cultural competence and critical consciousness—not merely performance.

Shawn Ginwright (2018), in his model of healing-centered engagement, offers a more expansive vision of success—one that centers emotional well-being, relational connection, and joy. It's not just the absence of trauma but the presence of possibility.

So let's ask different questions:

- How many students felt safe enough to come out this year?
- How many classrooms displayed student-created art centering queer joy?
- How often did adults apologize and repair harm when they got it wrong?
- How many caregivers cried tears of relief because someone *finally* saw their child?

Let's stop measuring survival. Let's start measuring freedom.

Braving Forward: Big and Small Acts of Transformative Courage

There is no one way to BRAVE forward.

Some acts of courage are televised. Others happen in the quiet of an IEP meeting, a bus ride, or a one-on-one hallway conversation. Some make headlines. Others just make a child feel seen for the first time.

The work of creating brave spaces for LGBTQIA+ youth is as diverse as the educators, leaders, caregivers, and community partners called to do it. And no matter who you are or where you serve, this work belongs to you.

Let's imagine what it looks like to BRAVE forward through multiple lenses.

For Early Career Educators

You may not feel like you have power yet—but you do. You carry fresh eyes and a deep well of empathy. You are close to the classroom, to the conversations, to the culture.

Your BRAVE may look like

- Asking why gendered dress codes still exist.
- Building in LGBTQIA+ affirming books from day one.
- Starting a GSA—even if it's just two students.
- Correcting misgendering gently but firmly, even when senior staff are watching.

For Seasoned Educators (15+ Years)

You are culture carriers and system whisperers. You know how schools breathe—and how they get stuck. You've seen shifts and cycles. You may carry fatigue, but you also carry influence.

Your BRAVE may look like

- Modeling vulnerability by acknowledging past silence—and choosing differently now.
- Mentoring LGBTQIA+ or questioning educators.
- Challenging bias in staff meetings with both wisdom and grace.
- Holding the line when policy tries to roll back inclusion.

For Rural Educators

You may feel isolated, but you are never alone. Your work is urgent and deeply relational. In small towns, visibility is both radical and risky—but also deeply transformative.

Your BRAVE may look like

- Creating the first-ever "Safe Space" sign in your school building.
- Writing a local op-ed on LGBTQIA+ inclusion.
- Hosting a book club for staff that includes queer authors.
- Partnering with community organizations, even if they're miles away.

For Career Changers

You bring new wisdom, new language, and fresh courage. Whether you're coming from corporate, ministry, military, or nonprofit work, you are proof that evolution is possible.

Your brave may look like

- Naming your learning curve without shame.
- Using your outside perspective to ask bold, essential questions.
- Making visible connections between equity in the world and equity in the classroom.
- Advocating for the youth you *used to be.*

For Alternative Education and Special Educators

You work at the intersections of disability, trauma, race, language, and identity. You hold students who have already been pushed out. You are often their last lifeline.

Your brave may look like

- Creating trauma-informed, gender-inclusive classroom agreements.
- Integrating queer joy into individualized learning plans.
- Standing between students and systems that have harmed them.
- Advocating for policies that affirm intersecting identities.

For Educators Who Are Parents or Caregivers of LGBTQIA+ Youth

You carry this work home with you. Your child's safety, joy, and affirmation live alongside your advocacy. You are raising brave souls—and becoming one in the process.

Your brave may look like

- Navigating school systems with fierce love and accountability.
- Educating your child's educators.
- Creating the safe home you never had.
- Choosing visibility—for your child's future and your own healing.

For Community Partners (Coaches, After-School Providers, Faith Leaders, Social Workers, Case Managers)

You see youth in their unfiltered moments—when their guard is down and their truth is raw. You are their bridge, their buffer, their bonus adult.

Your brave may look like

- Interrupting homophobia in a locker room.
- Asking for a student's pronouns and meaning it.
- Creating spaces where students lead, heal, and rest.
- Becoming a voice in rooms educators don't often get to enter.

BRAVING Forward Is Consistent, Courageous Action

No matter your title, training, or timeline, there is a place for you in this work. Bravery is not a personality trait. It is a practice. It is not always loud, but it is always present.

Bravery looks like

- A teacher who changes their classroom library.
- A school nurse who defends a student's right to be called by their chosen name.
- A principal who chooses a policy rooted in justice instead of convenience.
- A student who comes out—and stays out.
- An ally who keeps going even after they get it wrong.

This Work Is Ours to Do: A Love Letter to the Future

Dear Beloved,

We've walked together through stories that hold pain and promise, language that liberates, and strategies that push beyond the safe into the sacred. If you're here—truly here—you already know this isn't just a book. It's an invitation. A mirror. A reminder. A map.

The future our youth deserve will not appear fully formed. It will be built—slowly, daily, imperfectly—by brave educators, students, caregivers, and leaders who dare to believe in a world more honest, more whole, and more humane than the one we inherited.

Bravery isn't about being fearless. It's about showing up *anyway.* For some of us, that will mean standing on podiums. For others, it will mean standing up in faculty meetings. For many, it will be standing beside a child who doesn't yet have the words for their identity—but knows you see them.

"We are the house of the rejected," Pray Tell once said in *Pose*.
"But today, we are the house of the respected."

Let us build that house.
Let us decorate it with an affirmation.
Let us secure its foundation with policy and practice.
Let us make its roof wide enough to shelter every kind of body, voice, story, and family.
Let us light its hallways with joy.
Let us guard its doors with fierce love.
Let us not wait for permission to protect our youth.
Let us remember: we are already the people we've been waiting for.

Bravely Yours,
Craig

Key Takeaways

- Bravery is not a one-size-fits-all identity—it's a daily practice rooted in presence, not perfection.
- Co-liberation means moving from performative allyship to collective transformation; we are not free until all of us are free.
- Educators, caregivers, and community members each have a role to play. BRAVE leadership happens at every level of the ecosystem.
- Liberation isn't measured by test scores but by safety, self-expression, cultural pride, and joy.
- Rest is not a retreat from the work—it is a radical practice that sustains justice, especially for those most affected.
- Visibility without policy is not enough. Affirming students in spirit also means affirming them in systems, curriculum, and care.
- Your past silence or fear does not disqualify you. You are allowed to begin again—and to keep becoming.

BRAVE Reflection Questions

Use these in staff meetings, journaling, or advisory spaces:

- **Belonging:** How do I create spaces—big and small—where LGBTQIA+ youth and colleagues feel rooted, welcomed, and celebrated?
- **Respect:** What behaviors, policies, or norms in my classroom or organization need to be disrupted in order to honor the dignity of all?
- **Advocacy:** What systems of harm can I challenge, audit, or reimagine—starting with my own role, position, or influence?
- **Visibility:** How do I show up in public and private ways that reflect my values? What messages am I sending—even when I say nothing?
- **Empathy:** When I've made mistakes, how do I repair harm? How do I hold space for others to grow and for myself to begin again?

Chapter 10 Playlist

Visit www.ccmeducationgroup.co/WeAreBraveEducators to access a curated library of tools, stories, and strategies to help you build your own brand of BRAVE:

- *Letter to My Younger Self* writing worksheet (personal reflection or group facilitation).
- *Braving Forward Matrix*: role-based self-assessment + action planning template (Early Career, Rural, Veteran, Special Ed, etc.).
- *Inclusive Policy Audit Checklist*: from dress codes to curriculum, a tool for shifting systems, not just signals.
- *Rest & Resistance Resource Pack*: practices from The Nap Ministry, adrienne maree brown, and Dr. Ginwright for healing-centered leadership.

Acknowledgments

To my Beloveds—the youth and grown folks alike—who trusted me with your stories, your scars, your sacred dreams for something better: thank you. You cracked open your truth and let me gather it with tender hands. You let me hold your hurt, your joy, your rage, and your radical hope. That's not something I take lightly. You didn't have to trust me—but you did. And I carry that trust like a drumbeat in my chest. This book is stitched with your brilliance and your bravery.

To my forever partner and divine reflection, Omari—my love, my rib, my balance. You are the soft place I land and the steady hand that holds me upright. You've taught me what unconditional Black queer love looks, feels, and sounds like—gentle, loud, freeing, and whole. Loving you is a sermon and a celebration. You've been my mirror when I didn't recognize myself and my megaphone when I needed to remember who I am. Thank you for teaching me how to show up *boldly, fully,* and *tenderly.*

To my parents—Mama and Daddy—thank you for doing the work, for stretching, for choosing love again and again. You loved me out loud, even when the world tried to quiet me. Your prayers worked. Your protection worked. Your embrace of *all of me* gave me wings. Because of you, I get to live in possibility and promise.

To my Godmothers, Alicia and Felicia—thank y'all for always seasoning your love with wisdom, laughter, and some good ol' New Orleans flavor. Y'all loved me through hard truths and high moments. You've been my spiritual compass, offering that gumbo blend of soul-deep clarity and homegrown care.

To my Brothers—Mikal, Marcel, Big Mike, Pierre, Michael B., Curtis S., Byron, Quincey, Corey Y., Dr. Brandon C., Dakarai, Derrick Y., Jonathan A., and Justice—y'all are branches of my soul. You've offered me Baldwin's sharp tongue, Hughes's quiet fire, Coogler's vision, and E. Lynn's heartbeat. You've shown up with a deep, unwavering brotherhood that holds me on the days when the world is too loud. Thank you for choosing me as your kin, again and again.

To the Sistahs and Soul Women who carried me when I couldn't carry myself—Shaplaie, Charisma, Chaunte, Chastity, Krista, Kim P., and Suzy—you are grace in motion. Y'all prayed for me, affirmed me, poured wisdom into my spirit, and checked me with love when I needed it most. You are the definition of truth telling and joy giving. Thank you for being my circle of light.

To Dr. David A. Johns, my Brother in brilliance and Black queer radiance—*you are a superhero in this world and in mine.* Your walk is a master class in justice, in tenderness, in strategic rebuke, and in holy disruption. You move through the world with a poetic defiance of white supremacy and a fierce protection of our people. You remind me that being Black, queer, and revolutionary isn't just possible—it's *divine.* Thank you for showing me that liberation looks like love wrapped in action.

And to Susan H., my editor and gentle guide—thank you for believing in me when I wasn't sure I believed in myself. Your thoughtful nudges, patient grace, and unwavering presence carried me through a season thick with doubt and drenched in a national storm designed to suppress, to silence, to erase our queer magic. But little do they know: our magic has always outlasted their hatred. The fact that this book is finding light is a *rebuke* of that erasure. You helped me carry this story through the fog, and I will forever be grateful for your trust and your tenderness.

And to every soul who has ever prayed for me, walked beside me, challenged me, or reminded me to rest: I see you. I thank you. I carry you with me.

This book?
It ain't just words on pages.
It's a love letter.
It's a call to arms.
It's a mirror and a megaphone.
And it's dedicated to *us.*
Because we do not get free alone. And we ain't finished yet.

References

Aarons-Martin, C. (2024, March 3). Protecting LGBTQ+ students from harm. *Educational Leadership.* https://www.ascd.org/el/articles/protecting-lgbtq-students-from-harm

ACLU. (2025). Legislative attacks on LGBTQ rights: 2025. American Civil Liberties Union. https://www.aclu.org/legislative-attacks-on-lgbtq-rights-2025Alford, K. (2024, May). Navigating the Black nuances: Analyzing and understanding the intersectional perspectives of Black transgender Arkansans utilizing Maslow's Hierarchy of Needs (Master's thesis, University of Arkansas, Fayetteville). Student Theses & Dissertations. ScholarWorks@UARK. https://scholarworks.uark.edu/etd/5360/

Alyami, H., & Ghamri, R. A. (2023). Professional support, efficacy beliefs, and compassion fatigue in principals during the COVID-19 pandemic. *International Journal of Educational Research Open, 5,* 100332.

American Psychological Association. (2024). Guidelines for psychological practice with sexual minority persons. https://www.apa.org/pi/lgbt/resources

American Public Health Association. (2024). LGBTQ students report: Safe and supportive school environments assessment. https://www.apha.org/getcontentasset/749b785b-5801-46fa-b746-475f323d3217/7ca0dc9d-611d-46e2-9fd3-26a4c03ddcbb/lgbtq_students_report_09-2024.pdf

Aniftos, R. (2022, June 30). Beyoncé unveils "Renaissance" cover and reveals her intention for the new album. *Billboard.* https://www.billboard.com/music/music-news/beyonce-renaissance-cover-art-new-album-intention-1235109273/

Artz, S. (2001). When GI Joe meets Barbie. *Journal of Child and Youth Care Work, 15,* 15–29.

Bailey, M. M. (2013). *Butch queens up in pumps: Gender, performance, and ballroom culture in Detroit.* University of Michigan Press. https://doi.org/10.3998/mpub.799908

Bennett, J. (2023, March 28). "Consider this the home base": State commission on LGBTQ youth hosts rally ahead of Trans Day of Visibility. *WGBH News.* https://www.wgbh.org/news/local/2023-03-28/consider-this-the-home-base-state-commission-on-lgbtq-youth-hosts-rally-ahead-of-trans-day-of-visibility

Beyoncé. (2022). *Renaissance* [Album]. Parkwood Entertainment; Columbia Records. https://open.spotify.com/album/6FJxoadUE4JNVwWHghBwnb

Bigelow, B. (2022, June 1). Teaching the fight for queer liberation. *Rethinking Schools*. https://rethinkingschools.org/articles/teaching-the-fight-for-queer-liberation/

Bose, N., & Chiacu, D. (2025, February 21). Trump, Maine's Democratic governor clash at White House over transgender athletes. *Reuters*. https://www.reuters.com/world/us/trump-maine-governor-clash-over-transgender-athletes-2025-02-21

Bozard, A. (2023). A systematic review of LGBTQ educators' experiences and LGBTQ curriculum in K–12 US public schools. *Multicultural Education Review, 14*(2), 1–19.

Brown, B. (2017). Finding our way to true belonging. *TED Ideas*. https://ideas.ted.com/finding-our-way-to-true-belonging/

Brown, B. (2021). *Atlas of the heart: Mapping meaningful connection and the language of human experience*. Random House.

Burga, S. (2025a, February 6). David J. Johns won't stop fighting for queer Black youth. *TIME*. https://time.com/7210619/david-j-johns-national-black-justice-collective/

Burga, S. (2025b, June 18). Supreme Court upholds gender-affirming-care ban: Here's what to know. *Time*. https://time.com/7295695/supreme-court-skrmetti-transgender-healthcare-minors/

Burk, T. J.-K. (2015). *Let the record show: Mapping queer art and activism in New York City, 1986–1995* (Doctoral dissertation, CUNY Graduate Center). CUNY Academic Works. https://academicworks.cuny.edu/cgi/viewcontent.cgi?article=1533&context=gc_etds

Cabrera, A. (2025, May 6). Salt Lake City adopts new banners, sidestepping pride flag ban. *Utah News Dispatch*. https://utahnewsdispatch.com/2025/05/06/salt-lake-city-adopts-new-banners-sidestepping-pride-flag-ban/

Callahan, M. (2018, April 19). The autistic, non-binary, queer, law student fighting for disability justice. *Northeastern University News*. https://news.northeastern.edu/2018/04/19/the-autistic-non-binary-queer-law-student-fighting-for-disability-justice/

CDC. (2023). Youth risk behavior survey data summary & trends report: 2011–2021. https://www.cdc.gov/healthyyouth/data/yrbs/index.htm

Cheves, A., & López, Q. (2025, June 16). 9 LGBTQ+ people explain how they love, hate, and understand the word "queer." *Them*. https://www.them.us/story/what-does-queer-mean

Combahee River Collective. (1977). The Combahee River Collective statement. BlackPast.org. https://www.blackpast.org/african-american-history/combahee-river-collective-statement-1977/

Conron, K. J. (2022, May 13). LGBT youth population in the United States. *Williams Institute*. https://williamsinstitute.law.ucla.edu/publications/lgbt-youth-pop-us/

Crenshaw, K. (1991). Mapping the margins: Intersectionality, identity politics, and violence against women of color. *Stanford Law Review, 43*(6), 1241–1299.

Davis, J. T. M., & Hines, M. (2020). How large are gender differences in toy preferences? A systematic review and meta-analysis of toy preference research. *Archives of Sexual Behavior, 49*(2), 373–394. https://doi.org/10.1007/s10508-019-01624-7

Deml, J., & Salk, A. (2025, June 22). Local support shines through at Clark County Pride Festival. *KOIN 6 News*. https://www.koin.com/local/clark-county/local-support-shines-through-at-clark-county-pride-festival/

Ditsworth, D. (2001). The portrayal of gender in the children's television program Sesame Street and its effect on the intended audience. *Atlantic Journal of Communication, 9*(2), 214–226. https://doi.org/10.1080/15456870109367410 researchgate.net

Ensz, M. R. (2021). Compassion fatigue among educators: A mixed methods study (Doctoral dissertation, Andrews University). Andrews University Digital Commons. https://digitalcommons.andrews.edu/cgi/viewcontent.cgi?article=3114&context=dissertations

Feeney, S., Freeman, N. K., & Schaffer, K. (2019, November). Focus on ethics: Gender expression and identity. National Association for the Education of Young Children. Retrieved from https://www.naeyc.org/resources/pubs/yc/nov2019/gender-expression-identity

Fields, A. (2025, June 18). Supreme Court shuts down access to healthcare for transgender youth in 27 states, strengthening legal hurdles in the fight for LGBTQ+ rights. Human Rights Campaign. https://www.hrc.org/press-releases/supreme-court-shuts-down-access-to-healthcare-for-transgender-youth-in-27-states-strengthening-legal-hurdles-in-the-fight-for-lgbtq-rights

Ginwright, S. (2018). The future of healing: Shifting from trauma informed care to healing centered engagement. https://ginwright.medium.com/the-future-of-healing-shifting-from-trauma-informed-care-to-healing-centered-engagement-634f557ce69c

GLSEN. (2024). The 2024 national school climate survey: The experiences of LGBTQIA2S+ youth in U.S. K–12 schools. https://www.glsen.org/research/2024-national-school-climate-survey

Greytak, E. A., Kosciw, J. G., & Zongrone, A. D. (2021). Supporting safe and inclusive schools for transgender students: A research brief. GLSEN. https://www.glsen.org

Guerra, C. (2025). Pride, 'No Kings', combine in Boston for march and festival. WBUR. https://www.wbur.org/news/2025/06/14/pride-no-kings-boston-march-festival

Gunn, A., & Clark, C. (2022). A systematic review of research on LGBTQ educators' experiences and LGBTQ curriculum in K–12 U.S. public schools. *Multicultural Education Review, 14*(2), 1–19. https://www.researchgate.net/publication/361504726_A_systematic_review_of_research_on_LGBTQ_educators'_experiences_and_LGBTQ_curriculum_in_K-12_US_public_schools

Hammond, Z. (2014). *Culturally responsive teaching and the brain: Promoting authentic engagement and rigor among culturally and linguistically diverse students* (2nd ed.). Corwin.

Hartman, S. (2020, October 19). How Saidiya Hartman retells the history of Black life. *The New Yorker*. https://www.newyorker.com/magazine/2020/10/26/how-saidiya-hartman-retells-the-history-of-black-life

The Heritage Foundation. (2023). *Mandate for leadership: The conservative promise—Project 2025.* https://static.heritage.org/project2025/2025_MandateForLeadership_FULL.pdf

Heubeck, E. (2025, January 27). Why boys don't want to become teachers, and what schools can do about it. *Education Week*. https://www.edweek.org/leadership/why-boys-dont-want-to-become-teachers-and-what-schools-can-do-about-it/2025/01

Human Rights Campaign. (2021). An epidemic of violence 2021: Fatal violence against the transgender and gender non-conforming community in 2021. https://www.hrc.org/resources/fatal-violence-against-the-transgender-and-gender-non-conforming-community-in-2021

Human Rights Campaign. (2023). 2023 LGBTQ+ youth report: The experiences and perspectives of LGBTQ+ youth in the United States. *HRC Foundation*. https://reports.hrc.org/2023-lgbtq-youth-report

Human Rights Campaign. (2024a). 2024 state equality index: A review of state legislation impacting LGBTQ people. https://www.hrc.org/resources/state-equality-index

Human Rights Campaign. (2024b). Welcoming schools annual report 2025. https://reports.hrc.org/welcoming-schools-annual-report-fy25

Human Rights Campaign. (2025, June 3). *Supreme Court shuts down access to healthcare for transgender youth in 27 states, strengthening legal hurdles in the fight for LGBTQ+ rights* [Press release]. https://www.hrc.org/press-releases/p2

Human Rights Campaign. (n.d.). A parent's quick guide for in-school transitions: Empowering families and schools to support transgender and non-binary students. https://hrc-prod-requests.s3-us-west-2.amazonaws.com/assets/ParentsGuideForSchoolTransitions.pdf

Kean, E.. (2020): Advancing a critical trans framework for education. *Curriculum Inquiry*. https://transreads.org/wp-content/uploads/2022/03/2022-03-05_62237b04e3b86_advancingacriticaltransframeworkforeducationelikean.pdf

Kosciw, J. G., Clark, C. M., Truong, N. L., & Zongrone, A. D. (2022). The 2021 national school climate survey: Key findings. GLSEN. https://www.glsen.org/research

Ladson-Billings, G. (1995). Toward a theory of culturally relevant pedagogy. *American Educational Research Journal, 32*(3), 465–491. https://lmcreadinglist.pbworks.com/f/Ladson-Billings%20%281995%29.pdf

Lambda Legal. (2024). Legal protections for LGBTQ+ families and youth across the U.S. https://www.lambdalegal.org

Levin, S. (2023, June 23). 'Get off our backs and let us live': Miss Major is still fighting for trans rights after 50 years of resistance. *The Guardian*. https://www.theguardian.com/us-news/2023/jun/22/miss-major-trans-activist-lgbtq-rights-interview

Levin, S. (2025, May 2). Win for Maine as Trump officials agree to halt school funding freeze. *The Guardian*. https://www.theguardian.com/us-news/2025/may/02/trump-maine-funding-freeze

Love, B. (2019). *We want to do more than survive: Abolitionist teaching and the pursuit of educational freedom*. Beacon Press.

Marchese, D. (2023, July 27). Alok Vaid-Menon is "fighting for trans ordinariness" [Interview by D. Marchese; Photograph by M. Doumbouya]. *The New York Times Magazine*. https://www.nytimes.com/interactive/2023/07/29/magazine/alok-vaid-menon-interview.html

Marrun, N. A. (2022). A transgender studies approach for educators in schools: Reflections on cissexist pitfalls, bifurcated frameworks, and racial justice. *Teachers College Record, 124*(8). DOI:10.1177/01614681221121514

Massachusetts Commission on LGBTQ Youth. (2025). Safe Schools Program for LGBTQ students. Mass.gov. https://www.mass.gov/info-details/safe-schools-program-for-lgbtq-students

McCauley, L. (2025, February 21). In heated exchange over trans rights, Gov. Mills tells President Trump: 'See you in court' — President Donald Trump singled out Maine for not complying with executive order on transgender athletes. *Maine Morning Star*. https://mainemorningstar.com/2025/02/21/gov-mills-said-maine-will-not-be-bullied-into-complying-with-trumps-transgender-athlete-order

Mendoza, K., & Johnson, C. C. (2024). A (TRANS)formative approach to gender-inclusive science education. *Journal of Research in Science Teaching, 61*(4), 937–971. https://doi.org/10.1002/tea.21928

Modan, N. (2024, July 17). California becomes first state to prohibit schools from outing LGBTQ+ students. *K–12 Dive*. www.k12dive.com/news/california-first-state-prohibit-schools-from-outing-LGBTQ-students/721576/

Moran, P. (2023). Do we belong? Promoting a sense of belonging in LGBTQ youth through artistic community engagement: A literature review [Master's thesis, Lesley University]. Lesley University DigitalCommons. https://digitalcommons.lesley.edu/cgi/viewcontent.cgi?article=1628&context=expressive_theses

Movement Advancement Project. (2024). LGBTQ issues in education. https://www.mapresearch.org/policy-and-issue-analysis/education

Muhammad, G. (2020). *Cultivating genius: An equity framework for culturally and historically responsive literacy*. Scholastic.

Muhammad, G. (2023). *Unearthing joy: A guide to culturally and historically responsive teaching and learning*. Scholastic.

Mulvihill, G. (2025, August 1). States sue Trump, saying he is intimidating hospitals over gender-affirming care for youth. *Associated Press*. https://apnews.com/article/dfc156f4bffcf4b6136658207488d17d

National AIDS Memorial. (2020). The AIDS Memorial Quilt. https://www.aidsmemorial.org/quilt

National Black Justice Coalition. (2024, June 28). NBJC condemns SCOTUS decision to uphold Tennessee's ban on gender-affirming care for transgender youth. https://nbjc.org/nbjc-condemns-scotus-decision-to-uphold-tennessees-ban-on-gender-affirming-care-for-transgender-youth/

National Education Association. (n.d.). LGBTQ+ support and protection. https://www.nea.org/advocating-for-change/racial-social-justice/tools-justice/lgbtq-support-protection

Ohito, E. O. (2024). The white silence(r): Noticing the sonics of whiteness on the anti-racist teacher education landscape. *Teaching and Teacher Education, 144,* Article 104570. https://doi.org/10.1016/j.tate.2024.104570

Paceley, M. S., Sattler, P., Goffnett, J., & Jen, S. (2020). "It feels like home": Transgender youth in the Midwest and conceptualizations of community climate. *Journal of Community Psychology, 48*(6), 1863–1881.

Padayachee, A., & Kriger, S. (2024). Decolonizing classroom management: A critical examination of the cultural assumptions and norms in traditional practices. In *A collaborative approach of Ubuntu: Dismantling colonial classroom management practices in South African schools through the spirit of Ubuntu* (p. 147). Rowman & Littlefield.

Pfister, T., Rimm-Kaufman, S., & Sandilos, L. E. (2025, June 26). What middle schoolers can teach us about empathy. University of Virginia School of Education and Human Development. https://education.virginia.edu/news-stories/what-middle-schoolers-can-teach-us-about-empathy

PFLAG. (n.d.). When your child comes out. https://pflag.org/resource/parents-comingout/

Pinckney, A.-N. (2021). *Intersecting spaces: A narrative inquiry of queer, Black, Indigenous, people of color in higher education* (Master's thesis, California State University). California State University ScholarWorks. https://scholarworks.calstate.edu/downloads/wp988s97j

Queer Youth Assemble. (2023). QYA list of demands. Outright Vermont. https://www.documentcloud.org/documents/23736779-qya-list-of-demands/

Reign, E. (2018, August 21). These filmmakers are making sure Marsha P. Johnson's legacy lives on forever. *them.* https://www.them.us/story/happy-birthday-marsha-interview

Renold, E. (2004). *Girls, boys and junior sexualities: Exploring childrens' gender and sexual relations in the primary school* (1st ed.). Routledge.

Reynolds, D. (2025, January 3). Civil rights leader David Johns is fighting to reclaim the future for Black queer America. *LGBTQ Nation.* https://www.lgbtqnation.com/2025/01/civil-rights-leader-david-johns-is-fighting-to-reclaim-the-future-for-black-queer-america/

Riedel, S. (2025, May 5). Maine governor secures school lunch victory in fight with Trump over trans athletes — The U.S. Department of Agriculture will unfreeze $2 million in nutrition funding as part of a settlement. *Them.* https://www.them.us/story/maine-janet-mills-school-lunch-funding-trump-administration-feud

Roberts, C. J. (2025, June 18). *United States v. Skrmetti, No. 23-477, 605 U.S.* https://www.supremecourt.gov/opinions/24pdf/23-477_2cp3.pdf

Schapitl, L. (2025, February 21). 'See you in court': Trump and Maine's governor spar over trans athlete order. *NPR.* https://www.wunc.org/2025-02-21/see-you-in-court-trump-and-maines-governor-spar-over-trans-athlete-order

Shammas, B., Chu, H., & Swenson, K. (2025, June 8). Rally and march on the National Mall cap WorldPride events in D.C. *The Washington Post.* https://www.washingtonpost.com/dc-md-va/2025/06/08/world-pride-rally-march-national-mall/

Skerry, P. (2021). Why "Black Lives Matter" matters. *National Affairs, 47.* https://www.nationalaffairs.com/publications/detail/why-black-lives-matter-matters

Smallens, Y. (2024, May 10). School officials should protect trans youth, not "out" them [Commentary]. *The Progressive. Human Rights Watch.* https://www.hrw.org/news/2024/05/10/school-officials-should-protect-trans-youth-not-out-them

Smallens, Y. (2025, June 3). "They're ruining people's lives": Bans on gender-affirming care for transgender youth in the U.S. *Human Rights Watch.* https://www.hrw.org/report/2025/06/03/theyre-ruining-peoples-lives/bans-gender-affirming-care-transgender-youth-us

Smith, A. (2010). Queer theory and Native studies: The heteronormativity of settler colonialism. *GLQ: A Journal of Lesbian and Gay Studies, 16*(1–2), 41–68. https://doi.org/10.1215/10642684-2009-012

Smith, L. C., Simpfenderfer, A. D., Garnett, B. R., Knox, P. N., & Kervick, C. T. (2025). A restorative attempt to bend the binary: The experiences of genderqueer students in a restorative school district. *Educational Researcher, 54*(4), 188–200. https://doi.org/10.3102/0013189X251316853

Sojoyner, D. (2013). Black radicals make for bad citizens: Undoing the myth of the school to prison pipeline. *Berkeley Review of Education, 4*(2). https://doi.org/10.5070/B84110021

Stone, W., & Simmons-Duffin, S. (2025, January 31). Trump administration purges websites across federal health agencies. *NPR.* https://www.npr.org/sections/shots-health-news/2025/01/31/nx-s1-5282274/trump-administration-purges-health-websites

Taylor, K.-Y. (2020, July 20). Until Black women are free, none of us will be free. *The New Yorker.* https://www.newyorker.com/news/our-columnists/until-black-women-are-free-none-of-us-will-be-free

The Trevor Project. (2023a). National survey on LGBTQ youth mental health 2023. https://www.thetrevorproject.org/survey-2023/

The Trevor Project. (2023b). The impact of houselessness and food insecurity on the mental health of LGBTQ young people. https://www.thetrevorproject.org/research-briefs/the-impact-of-houselessness-and-food-insecurity-on-the-mental-health-of-lgbtq-young-people/

The Trevor Project. (2023c). Positive events and mental health among LGBTQ young people. https://www.thetrevorproject.org/research-briefs/positive-events-and-mental-health-among-lgbtq-young-people/

The Trevor Project. (2024a, March 4). Closed: Trump admin officially shuts down the 988 Suicide & Crisis Lifeline's LGBTQ youth specialized services. https://www.thetrevorproject.org/blog/closed-trump-admin-officially-shuts-down-the-988-suicide-crisis-lifelines-lgbtq-youth-specialized-services/

The Trevor Project. (2024b, June 28). Supreme Court greenlights healthcare discrimination for transgender youth in U.S. v. Skrmetti. https://www.thetrevorproject.org/blog/supreme-court-greenlights-healthcare-discrimination-for-transgender-youth-in-u-s-v-skrmetti/

The Trevor Project. (2024c). 2024 U.S. national survey on the mental health of LGBTQ+ young people. https://www.thetrevorproject.org/survey-2024/

The Trevor Project. (2025). Closed: Trump admin officially shuts down the 988 Suicide & Crisis Lifeline's LGBTQ+ youth specialized services. https://www.thetrevorproject.org/blog/closed-trump-admin-officially-shuts-down-the-988-suicide-crisis-lifelines-lgbtq-youth-specialized-services/

Uber, E. (2025, May 17). Art installation on National Mall shares trans voices of hope, defiance. *The Washington Post.* https://www.washingtonpost.com/dc-md-va/2025/05/17/freedom-to-be-trans-quilt-aclu

Villarreal, Y. (2018, July 20). 'Pose': FX drama about 1980s underground ball scene is a big step for trans community, producer says. *Los Angeles Times.* https://www.latimes.com/entertainment/tv/la-et-st-pose-feature-20180720-story.html

Wagaman, M. A., Shelton, J., Carter, R., & McDaniel, M. (2022). Building empathy in social work practice: A grounded theory of LGBTQ+ youth engagement. *Frontiers in Psychology, 13,* Article 8906061. https://doi.org/10.3389/fpsyg.2022.8906061

Will, M. (2020, January 14). LGBTQ teachers await decision on discrimination protections. *Education Week*. https://www.edweek.org/policy-politics/lgbtq-teachers-await-decision-on-discrimination-protections/2020/01

World Health Organization. (n.d.). Gender and health. WHO Health Topics. https://www.who.int/health-topics/gender

Yale University. (n.d.). LGBTQIA+ health: Home. Harvey Cushing/John Hay Whitney Medical Library. https://guides.library.yale.edu/LGBTQHealth

Yeh, K. (2023, September 7). How I fought for trans justice this summer. *ACLU*. https://www.aclu.org/news/lgbtq-rights/how-i-fought-for-trans-justice-this-summer

Young, J. (2025, January 22). A guide for parents of LGBTQ+ youth in 2025. *Brave Trails*. https://www.bravetrails.org/blog/a-guide-for-parents-of-lgbtq-youth-in-2025

Zak, P. J. (2015). Why inspiring stories make us react: The neuroscience of narrative. *Cerebrum*. https://pmc.ncbi.nlm.nih.gov/articles/PMC4445577/

Index

The letter *f* following a page locator denotes a figure.

About the Author

Craig Aarons-Martin (he/him) is an award-winning Black queer educator, author, and consultant whose life and leadership are rooted in equity, belonging, and liberation. With more than two decades of service in education—as teacher, principal, superintendent, and district leader—Craig has built a legacy of creating spaces where young people can show up fully in their truth.

His leadership has been nationally recognized, including honors as the 2018 National Distinguished Principal by the National Association of Elementary School Principals, Massachusetts Elementary Principal of the Year, and Boston Public Schools Educator of the Year. These awards reflect his courage in cultivating school cultures that affirm identity, advance equity, and foster joy.

Craig is CEO of CCM Education Group, partnering with schools, districts, companies, and community organizations to cocreate solutions in leadership, equity, and organizational change. His consulting and thought leadership emphasize the power of identity, healing, and joy as essential to building communities where LGBTQIA+ youth are not only protected but also celebrated.

As an active ASCD Faculty member, Craig has shaped the organization's work for more than a decade. He was named an ASCD Emerging Leader (2012) and has served as an affiliate leader for Emerging Leaders and Massachusetts ASCD, a reviewer for books and conference proposals, and a co-designer of the ASCD Emerging Leader Mentoring Program. He has served on the ISTE+ASCD 2025 Conference Planning Committee and played a key role in the inaugural 2024 ASCD + Ghana International Education Summit.

Craig's writing has appeared in *Education Week, K12 Digest,* and *Educational Leadership* magazine, including "Protecting LGBTQ Students from Harm." He is also an adjunct professor at the University of Massachusetts–Lowell, where he prepares the next generation of educational leaders.

His advocacy is grounded in his lived experience as a queer Black man and in his marriage to Omari Aarons-Martin, which roots him in the values of love, resilience, and authenticity. Across every role, Craig remains committed to advancing transformational leadership and building schools where courage, collaboration, and liberation thrive.

Related ISTE+ASCD Resources

At the time of publication, the following resources were available (ASCD stock numbers in parentheses).

The Consciously Unbiased Educator by Huda Essa (#121014)

Educating for Justice: Schoolwide Strategies to Prepare Students to Recognize, Analyze, and Challenge Inequity by Scott Seider, Aaliyah El-Amin, and Julia Bott (#124009)

The EQ Way: How Emotionally Intelligent School Leaders Navigate Turbulent Times by Ignacio Lopez (#123046)

Finding Your Leadership Soul: What Our Students Can Teach Us About Love, Care, and Vulnerability by Carlos R. Moreno (#123025)

Fix Injustice, Not Kids and Other Principles for Transformative Equity Leadership by Paul Gorski and Katy Swalwell (#120012)

Meet Their Needs, and They'll Succeed: Transforming Students' Lives Through Positive Relationships by Salome Thomas-EL (#121003)

The Teens Are Not Alright: School and Classroom Practices to Support Student Well-Being by Cathy Vatterott (#126001)

The Way to Inclusion: How Leaders Create Schools Where Every Student Belongs by Julie Causton, Kate MacLeod, Kristie Pretti-Frontczak, Jenna Mancini Rufo, and Paul Gordon (#123001)

We Belong: 50 Strategies to Create Community and Revolutionize Classroom Management by Laurie Barron and Patti Kinney (#122002)

For up-to-date information about ISTE+ASCD resources, go to iste-ascd.org. You can search the complete archives of *Educational Leadership at ascd.org/ el. To contact us, send an email to memsupport@iste-ascd.org or call 1-800-933-2723 or 703-578-9600.*

www.ingramcontent.com/pod-product-compliance
Lightning Source LLC
LaVergne TN
LVHW080847170826
845678LV00006B/1731

* 9 7 8 1 4 1 6 6 3 4 5 3 9 *